RAISED ON PORN

Raised on Porn

© 2022 Benjamin Nolot
Published by Magic Lantern Press
(an imprint of Exodus Cry Inc.)

LCCN: 2022918917

ISBN 979-8-9850109-0-9 (paperback)
ISBN 979-8-9850109-1-6 (ePub)

22 23 24 25 26 27 | IS | 10 9 8 7 6 5 4 3 2 1

PRAISE FOR *RAISED ON PORN:*

Understanding what it means to grow up in a misogynist porn culture requires a level of nuance, compassion, and empathy that porn often obliterates. *Raised on Porn* not only forces us to take an unflinching look at porn culture, but it also provides an analysis of the harms of porn—which mobilizes activism against an industry that is reshaping the social, emotional, and cognitive map of young people in ways that undermine healthy development, women's equality, and a sustainable culture.

—GAIL DINES, PhD
Professor Emerita, Wheelock College
CEO and President, Culture Reframed

In *Raised on Porn*, Benjamin Nolot covers the difficult and complex topic of pornography from a multifaceted perspective. He describes how pornography affects our brains by detailing the latest neuroscience. He also covers how porn permeates and taints every aspect of our culture. The take-home message from this powerful book is that porn impacts much more than our sexuality; it destroys our empathic core, our very humanity. All who take time to carefully read this important book will be educated, but more importantly, will be motivated and empowered to change this increasingly confused world.

—DONALD L. HILTON JR., MD
Neurosurgeon

Raised on Porn is a powerful new weapon in the growing arsenal of evidence against the destructive, deforming, and diabolical harms of the global industrial porn complex. This book blows apart the porn industry's PR spin that its product is mere fantasy. It is an excellent resource for anyone interested in understanding the evidence of harm.

—MELINDA TANKARD REIST
Senior Lecturer, Centre for Ethics and Culture
University of Notre Dame, Sydney

Raised on Porn refuses to look away from the pornography industry's exploitation of women and the corrosive nature of the images it produces. These brutal realities are hard to face, especially when our patriarchal society so often celebrates pornography as sexual liberation. But a healthy sexuality is possible only if we follow Benjamin Nolot's courageous example in this book—the example of shining a light on these dark realities.

—ROBERT JENSEN, PhD
Professor Emeritus, University of Texas
Author of *Getting Off: Pornography and the End of Masculinity*

In *Raised on Porn*, Benjamin Nolot presents an unflinching look at the harms of porn. He relies on a bevy of data, experts, and interviews with porn consumers and producers as evidence that porn is a pressing public health crisis. *Raised on Porn* is an empirical rejection of the conflation of pornography with sexual freedom. It is a must-read book for every parent and every person who gives porn a pass.

—CAROLINE HELDMAN, PhD
Chair of the Politics Department, Occidental College
Executive Director, Represent Pledge
Research Director, Geena Davis Institute on Gender in Media

Pornography is normalizing an extreme version of the teaching that women are sexual objects for men, the property of men, and that they have less value than men. This teaching not only lays a foundation for epidemic levels of violence and discrimination against women and girls to persist, but it also ultimately encourages men and boys to disconnect from their own humanity. In *Raised on Porn*, Benjamin Nolot has shined a revealing spotlight that will elevate your awareness and deepen your understanding of porn culture.

—TONY PORTER
CEO, A Call to Men
NFL, NBA, NHL, and MLB advisor

This book is a tour de force that engages the history, science, and biblical principles that must be named if we are to understand the scourge of pornography. Benjamin Nolot is a passionate, wise, and tender warrior who writes to free us from darkness and enable us to stand against the spirits of this age. The believing community can no longer hide from this heartache, and this book is a gift of enormous proportion to give us freedom, knowledge, and courage.

—DAN B. ALLENDER, PhD
Professor of Counseling Psychology and Founding President
The Seattle School of Theology & Psychology

Raised on Porn effectively exposes the truth behind the porn fallacy. Today's world is hardwired for hardcore porn, and this book elucidates the adult film industry's obscene nature and adequately expresses multifarious motivations for its end.

—JAN VILLARUBIA
Former adult film performer

With an eye on personal and cultural healing and liberation, Benjamin Nolot has taken up the enormous challenge of writing a deeply informative and compassionate book on pornography and pornography addiction. Using a wide-angle lens, *Raised on Porn* courageously and creatively addresses almost all of the important central and peripheral elements related to this complex and controversial subject. This book offers extremely useful and specific guidance for healing and for reclaiming one's own sexuality, relationships, and sanity from the domination and control of the pornography industry. Beyond all of these accomplishments, this valuable resource offers clarity, hope, and inspiration for living with integrity, respect, and mutuality.

—HARVEY SCHWARTZ, PhD
Author and Clinical Psychologist

Equally methodical and morally challenging, *Raised on Porn* bridges science and health on one hand, and human rights and dignity on the other. This study makes a significant contribution to citizens', researchers', and policy makers' understanding of the issue. It looks at how the brain, the market, and the internet are all wired—and what can't be changed and what can and must.

—AMB. (RET.) MARK P. LAGON, PhD
Distinguished Senior Scholar, Georgetown University,
Former director of the Office to Monitor and Combat Trafficking in Persons (for the US Department of State)
Former CEO of Polaris Project (an anti-trafficking non-profit)

BENJAMIN NOLOT

RAISED ON PORN

HOW PORN IS AFFECTING OUR LIVES AND WHAT WE CAN DO ABOUT IT

MAGIC LANTERN
PRESS

ORANGE COUNTY, CALIFORNIA

This book is dedicated
to everyone who has suffered
loss as a result of pornography's
detrimental impact.

I wrote in hopes of reclaiming
what has been stolen from us—
our dignity, our sexuality,
our very humanity.

CONTENTS

SECTION TWO

A WORD ABOUT SEX

As you have probably gathered, this is a book about modern porn.* The subject hits a nerve in our society because sex and sexuality impact everyone's life. It is a complicated topic, steeped in nuance and subjectivity. Because this book deals with subject matter that evokes a wide variety of strong opinions and vigorous debate, I provide the following brief framework through which we can understand human sexuality.

Sex is a beautiful, mysterious, powerful, and pleasurable form of communication, connection, and intimacy between individuals. Research has shown that healthy sexual engagement is highly beneficial for individuals and society. To many, it is sacred. Sex can promote robust relational connections. It can bond two people through the release of powerful neurochemicals, such as the "love hormone" oxytocin[1] and the so-called "monogamy molecule"[2] vasopressin. Sex can improve your physical health and even increase cognitive function and neuron growth in your brain.[3,4] It helps us emotionally by releasing hormones that reduce anxiety and stress.[5]

Beyond all that, sex can be downright exhilarating! Human sexuality is a vital part of what makes romantic relationships fulfilling and enjoyable. I am pro sex, even "sex positive" (but perhaps in a different

---

* I focus on heterosexual pornography, which constitutes the majority of mainstream porn today.

way than you are familiar with). I am committed to promoting a sexually healthy world—one where sex is enhancing to our well-being and rooted in empathy and mutuality.

However, to promote positive sexuality, we must juxtapose a healthy sexuality with its opposite: a toxic sexuality. The difference between the two is important to understand and imperative as a framework for the rest of this book, as we expose the unhealthy sexuality portrayed by mainstream pornography.

So, what is a definition of healthy sexuality that can be universally applied? The best way to understand a healthy human sexuality is through the lens of empathy and mutuality, combined with a "do no harm" ethical foundation.

I agree with author and researcher Dr. Meagan Tyler, who says that "sexual ethics assert that decisions can be made about what is right and wrong in regard to sexuality, which directly contradicts popular libertarian notions that all sexual expression is good in and of itself.... Sexual ethics recognize that sexual expression or pleasure which is contingent upon inequality or harm should be named as oppression rather than liberation." [6]

Indeed, mutuality is a necessary condition of any healthy sexual connection. Empathy should guide and govern all ethical affairs of humanity, especially our sexuality. Further, healthy sexual pleasure should not include harming another person. Anything that violates these principles is a form of sexual violation. As human beings, we possess a unique capacity for empathy—the ability to feel what another person is feeling, discern their emotions, and identify with their experiences. When we empathize with others, we become motivated by compassion to care for them. For most of us, brutalizing someone we empathize with is unthinkable. Instead, empathy inspires us to eliminate another person's suffering, or at least comfort him or her.

Without empathy, sexuality can take a dark turn. In-depth studies indicate that sex offenders suffer from a severe lack of empathy. Empathy helps us avoid harming one another, and it allows us to connect with and relate to each other on a deep emotional and existential level. Researcher Adena Galinsky (of the Johns Hopkins Bloomberg School of Public Health) revealed this about her research on empathy and sex: "How people interact and their ability to listen to each other and take each other's perspective can really influence the sex that they have." Her study analyzed data from more than 3,200 students, ages 18 to 26. "Our hypothesis is that empathetic individuals are more responsive to a partner's needs, and thus initiate a positive feedback cycle," she noted.[7]

Empathy helps us perceive another individual's needs, desires, comfort levels, pleasure, pain, happiness, or distress. It tunes us in to each other emotionally. It enables us to treat others with the care, tenderness, and compassion needed for a healthy and positive sexual encounter.

Mutuality is another hallmark of a healthy and ethical sexuality. When sex is approached with mutuality at its core, respect, dignity, and agency are the result. Authentic and enthusiastic consent is part of the equation, but mutuality transcends mere consent. Consent can be coerced, bribed, and manipulated in many ways. Mutuality, on the other hand, comes from a place of equal standing between two individuals.

Another way to describe mutuality is a reciprocity of desire. If your sexuality is governed by mutuality, you are concerned with your partner's desires as well as your own. When two people approach sex with mutuality, they experience deep sexual fulfillment, safety, and reciprocal respect.

Conversely, paid sex is not based on mutual desire. One person desires the sex, but the other doesn't. That's why payment is involved.

Because sex and desire are inextricably linked, paid sex is inherently devoid of mutuality. Paid sex is based on economic coercion. One person's rights supersede the rights of the other.

Authentic mutuality is devoid of all coercion—cultural, social, economic, psychological, relational, or circumstantial.

Finally, an ethical and healthy sexuality does no harm and causes no intentional injury or pain: emotional, mental, or physical. In fact, this kind of sexuality improves the health and well-being of both partners.

A sexuality guided by the principles above provides an ethical framework that protects personal autonomy and boundaries while creating plenty of room for creativity and shared pleasure. I call this kind of healthy sexuality *a relational sexuality*, or what author Andrea Dworkin calls a "humane sensuality based in equality." [8] In relational sexuality, both partners are seen, considered, respected, equal, and connected. This brand of sexual interaction can be playful, tender, exploratory, relationship-enhancing, intimate, spiritual, vulnerable, passionate, pleasurable, and shame-free. Relational sexuality humanizes us because it focuses on the whole person.

Mutual, relational sexuality stands in stark contrast with object sexuality. This brand of sexuality, a hallmark of porn, considers sex and one's sexual partner as a mere means to an end. It sees one's sexual partner as a masturbatory aid. It is based on taking, not giving or sharing. A sexual partner is a mirror, sponge, and receptacle—a collection of body parts that exist for the gratification of oneself.

Object sexuality is depersonalized, non-caring, and one-sided. It is laser-focused on a physical act to achieve the goal of "getting off," even at the other person's expense. It disregards the partner's desires, preferences, sexual history, emotions, pleasure, or needs.

Object sexuality is inhumane because it fails to consider the other person's humanity. It regards her or him as a mere "thing," to be conquered and used. Object sexuality ignores the fact that we are complex, sensitive, and multidimensional human beings.

This brings us to malevolent sexuality. This form of sexuality is based on the desire to violate or degrade the other person. It is a fusion of contempt and narcissistic sexuality. It takes pleasure in assaulting, humiliating, and tormenting. Malevolent sexuality is an attempt to dump extremely toxic emotional states on another person. This sexuality transfers one's own desperation, despair, anger, and humiliation to another human being. It can be vengeful to the point of taking pleasure in another's pain. One partner is a hostage to the sadistic tyranny of the other.

In each of the above models, power is used differently. In malevolent sexuality, power is used to destroy another person to achieve personal pleasure. In object sexuality, power is exercised to consume and use someone for personal pleasure.

Relational sexuality, by contrast, sees each partner striving to empower the other, with mutual pleasure as the goal.

We will return to this framework throughout the book, as we analyze and critique modern pornography.

THE GREAT INTERNET PORN EXPERIMENT

Currently, almost 60 percent of the world's population is online, including more than 90 percent of the US population.[9] People like former Google CEO Eric Schmidt predict that global internet saturation is coming soon. Even those who live in poor rural areas will not be left behind.[10] To that end, Google launched "Project Loon," a floating network of thousands of internet-transmitting balloons traveling on the edge of space, with the goal of bringing even the most remote areas online.[11] (Author's update: Although Loon was successful in bringing access to remote areas, the program was shut down due to a lack of commercial viability in early 2021.)

As part of his hope to "wire the world," Meta CEO Mark Zuckerberg's company has designed solar-powered unmanned aircraft that will beam the internet down to the masses from the sky.[12] Elon Musk has similar ambitions via his SpaceX company. He has launched more than 1,500 satellites throughout space, with the goal of bringing internet access to the entire planet.[13] Musk's plans include a partnership with Google Cloud, under which SpaceX's "Starlink" terminals will be planted at Google Cloud data centers. So, in a few years, everyone on planet Earth will have easy and free access to internet pornography.

The coming mass proliferation of internet pornography prompted Canadian psychologist and scientist Dr. Michael Seto to say, "We are in the midst of <u>the single largest unregulated social experiment in history</u>."[14]

This grand social experiment will reveal the consequences of nearly every child on earth growing up with hardcore violent porn as their primary source of sexual education. It will also reveal what happens to society when hypersexualized pornographic media becomes, in the words of scholar and author Dr. Gail Dines, "the wallpaper of our lives."[15]

The stakes are high, and given the impending ubiquity of internet pornography, we must take an inventory of porn's impact on our lives, the lives of our children, and our relationships, families, communities, and culture. We must also discover what can be done to repair and mitigate the damage porn causes. Doing so will enable us to understand and respond to the phenomenon of universal immersion into hardcore pornography.

To this end, I spent ten years on a quest to discover the truth about porn, its impact on us, and what we can do about it. I approached all of the content used in my analysis of pornography with <u>a public health and human rights framework</u>. I pored over mountains of peer-reviewed scientific journal articles, government reports, and nearly every book written on the subject, from the 1980s to today. I also went inside the porn industry to investigate how it operates. I interviewed some of the world's biggest porn producers, directors, and agents to get an inside look at how porn is created. I spoke face to face with current and former porn performers about their experiences in the industry.

In addition (and just as important), I spoke with neuroscientists, neurosurgeons, and psychologists about porn's impact on the brain. I talked with sociologists about porn's effects on society and relationships. I interviewed porn consumers who fell into lifetimes of addiction. I talked with couples who produce porn, and other couples whose relationships have been affected by it.

I asked sex-trafficking survivors about porn's role in their exploitation. I even spoke with survivors of CSAM: child sexual abuse material (previously called "child pornography"), and sex offenders. I spoke with those who advocate for porn and those who despise it, all in an effort to get a full understanding of a phenomenon that affects nearly all of our lives.

My goal for this book is to present a well-rounded, authentic, and truthful examination of the nature and impact of porn and to offer meaningful solutions to those who desire to overcome its harms. I am aware that this isn't a comfortable conversation, and I apologize in advance that some of the material I present will be graphic, often disturbing and heartbreaking. This was certainly the case for me as I traveled down the path of discovery. But understanding the truth about modern porn and the way it is impacting us is essential. Porn is unavoidable. Whether we like it or not, porn is a reality for this generation. The critical task at hand is to uncover the truth about porn and learn what we can do about it.

SECTION ONE

TRIGGER WARNING: The following chapters contain sexually explicit language. It has been used as thoughtfully and as sparingly as possible without compromising my ability to present an authentic and accurate representation of what pornography truly is.

1

A WORLD ON PORN

The *Sleep of One Hundred Years* is a Jewish folktale about a rabbi named Onias, who falls asleep on a hill overlooking Jerusalem and awakens 100 years later to a world he doesn't recognize. As he opens his eyes, he is stunned and puzzled by the world around him. He descends the hill into the city. The people look at him curiously. Some startle at the sight of him.

"Thou seemest like a creature from another world," someone says. As he roams the city in confusion, Onias regards everything as strange—the customs, the manners, and the habits of the people. They dress and speak differently.

Bewildered and disoriented, Onias pleads to be removed from the city and returned to the hill. "Lead me," he cries, "to the place of my long sleep. Perchance I will sleep again."

Now, imagine that you had fallen asleep 100 years ago and suddenly woken up today. You would open your eyes to a whole new world—drastically different from the one you remember. Imagine living in a time when most people traveled by foot, horse-drawn buggies, or trains. A time when lovers communicated by hand-written letters, and people gathered around radios for evening entertainment.

You would learn that rich people are flying into space, via their private companies. Everyday citizens drive electric cars, and people worldwide can communicate with one another via high-speed internet and smartphones.

If you fell asleep 100 years ago, you would have closed your eyes in an era when a person would be hard-pressed to find a sexually explicit image of any kind. But you would awaken to a world saturated in pornography. As you emerged from your slumber, you would see a world fundamentally altered by hypersexualized media—a world where human sexuality had been fundamentally redefined.

Most of us have been exposed to porn in one way or another. Academic studies report that between 93[16] and 100 percent[17] of boys, and between 62[18] and 82 percent[19] of girls are exposed to internet porn during their adolescence and young adulthood. Most young people will be exposed to pornography by age 13,[20] some even younger.[21] If you haven't been exposed yet, look at the person on your right and on your left. Statistics indicate that both of them have. The sheer amount of internet porn available today is difficult to comprehend, and that vast supply grows exponentially every year.

In 1991 there were fewer than 90 pornographic magazines published in the US. In 1997, there were about 900 pornographic sites on the web. By 2011, there were at least 2.5 million pornographic websites.[22] This explosion is due to the rise of the internet and the widespread use of high-tech devices.[23]

It is important to note that each website contains hundreds (if not thousands) of individual pages. That means that if there were 2.5 million porn websites in 2011, and if the average porn site hosted 500 individual pages or links, that's a yield of 1.25 billion pornographic web pages. And the scope of pornography available today far exceeds the 2011 numbers. One prominent site, YouPorn, proudly touts that they serve 4,000 pages per second during peak times, receiving more than 100 million page views per day.[24]

In 2019, Pornhub, one of the world's largest porn sites, received 42 billion visits: an average of 115 million visits every day. (According to Xbiz.com, daily visits had increased to 130 million by the time a 2020 "Tech Review" was published.)[25] To place this in context, that's like the populations of Canada, Australia, Poland, and the Netherlands all visiting at once.[26] In 2019 there were 39 billion searches performed on Pornhub; that is 8.7 billion more searches than in 2018.[27]

In 2019, Pornhub boasted that it had welcomed more than 6.8 million new video uploads. If you compiled all of that video content into one film and started watching it right now, you would still be watching in the year 2192![28] To deliver its high volume of explicit content, Pornhub's servers stream 209 gigabytes of data every second. For perspective, picture a 16GB USB thumb drive. Now imagine 194 million of those thumb drives, spanning 6,800 miles from end to end, or enough to traverse the circumference of the moon.[29]

While we're on the topic of mind-bending stats, Pornhub reports that they stream enough pornographic data to fill the storage of all of the world's iPhones.[30] These staggering numbers aren't just reserved for the best-known websites. Other porn sites, such as Xvideos, LiveJasmin, and Tube8, also receive billions of page views monthly.[31] According to author Gary Wilson, "Today a guy can see more hot babes in ten minutes than his ancestors could in several lifetimes."[32]

Singer John Mayer said (in an interview for *Playboy*) that pornography is "a new synaptic pathway. You wake up in the morning, open a thumbnail page, and it leads to a Pandora's box of visuals. There have probably been days when I saw three hundred vaginas before I got out of bed."[33]

Today, in the privacy of our bedrooms, we can access porn 24 hours a day, seven days a week, without paying a dime. Where and when did this porn explosion begin? Sexually explicit material has been sparsely available for generations, but pornography didn't enter the mainstream until after World War II. Until then, even Hollywood had conservative regulations that limited sexual content.[34] However, in 1948 a book was published, a book that would alter the course of human sexuality forever.

Alfred Kinsey, considered "the father of the sexual revolution," published *Sexual Behavior in the Human Male*, a "scientific study" of human sexuality. The conclusions cited in this first volume of "The Kinsey Reports" dramatically redefined the way society understood sex. (The second volume, titled *Sexual Behavior in the Human Female*, was published in 1953.)

"Kinsey not only studied sexuality," wrote one of his admirers, "he helped create it . . . in such a way that it is difficult to imagine what pre-1950s sexuality looked like."[35]

Although Kinsey's research methodology was eventually questioned and criticized, his reports were initially regarded as near-biblical truth. The general public had little idea of the flaws in the research. For example, at least one of his adult male research subjects admitted to having sexual contact with children. While Kinsey denied that he or any of his research team was involved in sexual experimentation on children—or trained anyone to observe children in inappropriate settings—his methodology raised the question of whether a researcher should obtain information from a sexual offender without notifying the police.

Further, his research indicated that 17 percent of "farm-bred males" had engaged in sexual intercourse with an animal,[36] which most people regarded as a suspiciously high number. Today, many people regard Kinsey's research as unreliable and unethical.

Unfortunately, his reports were originally regarded as science, so his conclusions were accepted. It is nearly impossible to overstate the impact that these reports had on the American public's psyche. In fact, many consider "The Kinsey Reports" to be the most influential publications of the 20th century.

When Kinsey reported that a majority of men (68 percent) reported having sex with a prostituted woman or that almost half of all married men had at least one affair,[37] the public was shocked. This was earth-shaking information for the American people, because it questioned everything we thought we knew about sexuality.

Five years after Kinsey's first report was published, a young Hugh Hefner arrived on the scene, ready to capitalize. Hefner confessed, "Kinsey had a tremendous impact on me. . . . [Kinsey's reports] supplied the evidence that proved the things that I had been feeling for so many years, which was that what we said about our sexuality was not what we did."[38] This was the validation Hefner needed to pursue his agenda of taking pornography from the "back street to the main street."[39] Hefner noted, "Kinsey was the researcher, and I was the pamphleteer."[40]

> "You wake up in the morning, open a thumbnail page, and it leads to a Pandora's box of visuals. There have probably been days when I saw three hundred vaginas before I got out of bed."
>
> JOHN MAYER, Singer-Songwriter

Thus, *Playboy* was born. In December of 1953, the first issue of *Playboy* was published. British journalist Christopher Turner reflected on that issue: "With an $8,000 loan ($1,000 from his mother, who had hoped he'd become a missionary), the 27-year-old Hefner produced a pasted-together magazine. He bought the rights to an old pin-up picture of Marilyn Monroe and used it as centerfold bait to drum up 70,000 advance orders."[41]

The caption describing Monroe's centerfold read, "She's as famous as Dwight Eisenhower and Dick Tracy, and she and Dr. Kinsey have monopolized sex this year." *Playboy* went on to become a colossal money-making enterprise that turned objectifying women's sexuality into an industry, an industry that changed the world as we know it.

By discovering the extremely lucrative commercial value of female sexuality, *Playboy* eventually inspired copycats like *Hustler* and *Penthouse*, which also experienced enormous financial success.

In the early to mid-1970s, porn entered the realm of film with a series of high-production movies such as *Deep Throat* and *Behind the Green Door,* ushering in "the Golden Age of Porn." Actor Warren Beatty took fellow performer Britt Ekland on a date to a porn film.[42] Porn became a cultural phenomenon. When the 1980s arrived, people began taking porn home with them in the form of VHS cassettes.

The 1990s brought us the World Wide Web, and the planet became hardwired with accessibility to endless pornographic images at the push of a button. The porn industry transformed from a handful of prominent magazines and pornographic film houses to an ocean of sexually explicit websites.

Today, porn is a multi-billion-dollar industry with an ever-increasing pool of customers. Theo Sapoutzis, former CEO and chairman of Adult Video News (AVN), the pornography industry's best-known trade journal, and organizer of the Adult Entertainment Expo (AEE), estimated that the pornography industry made roughly $10 billion in 2012.[43]

Current estimates are as high as $97 billion. In early 2019, *Relevant* magazine reported that three porn sites were among the 15 most popular in the United States, more popular than Instagram, Wikipedia, Twitter, Netflix, and ESPN.[44]

Thanks to the advent of "tube sites," porn has become more profitable than ever. Using the YouTube model, these sites are now cashing in on global porn consumption through paid advertising (and paid-content options). Porn has also invaded social media. Yes, with the advent of the internet, the levees were breached, the floodgates burst open, and porn and its influence came rushing like a violent river into almost every aspect of our lives. Technological advances like smartphones and tablets, streaming sites, and wireless connectivity have multiplied access to pornography, allowing it to be watched anonymously and for free.

Simply put, pornography is ubiquitous. In the words of one Playboy executive, "You're now one click away from every sex act imaginable for free."[45]

What does this mass proliferation of internet pornography mean for us? To answer that question, we must understand that porn isn't benign imagery coming to us via our various screens. Rather, it's a potent story about who we are as men and women—and the purpose of sex. And before we can fully understand porn's widespread impact, we must explore stories and their powerful influence on our lives, as individuals and as a society.

2

THE POWER OF STORY

*"Whoever tells the best story
shapes the culture."*

—ERWIN RAPHAEL McMANUS[46]

Humans are drawn to stories. Stories allow us to interpret our lives and share them with others. Stories provide us recognizable patterns in the midst of chaos. In these patterns, we find meaning. From the genesis of humankind, we have been telling stories. Hieroglyphics were inscribed by ancient Egyptians on the walls of darkened caves and tombs by firelight. Our ancestors told stories, purposefully passing down oral traditions from generation to generation. Stories were detailed on papyrus and parchment, transferred from one hand to another via carefully crafted scrolls.

Stories have always played an important role in human existence. Many people sacrificed their lives for the stories they believed in and the values those stories portrayed.

We need stories because they help us make sense of a confusing, complicated, and often painful existence. Through stories, we find the answers to life's big questions:

Who am I?

Why am I here?

What is right, and what is wrong?

Stories help us understand who we are and how we should live. They inspire us, comfort us, and connect us with people we've never met. They teach us about consequences. Stories show us the power of love, courage, compassion, and virtue—and the damaging effects of contempt, bitterness, greed, animosity, bigotry, revenge, and so much more. Because of their power to guide us, stories play a central role in developing shared values and forming social norms.

As we grow up, we are socialized by the stories that surround us. Socialization is the process of internalizing our culture's stories and developing our identity, worldview, and values. Stories play a central role in determining what we believe about ourselves and others. They have the power to build collective attitudes and beliefs—the shared values that form our culture.

As communications professor Sut Jhally is fond of saying, "Culture doesn't fall fully formed from heaven."[47] Instead, a culture is created, and story is a tool for constructing that culture. The socializing power of stories has serious implications, because as culture matures, it produces common attitudes, perceptions, ideals, and behaviors. These shared ideals and subsequent actions can be good or extremely evil.

The Triumph of the Will

Consider the story of Nazi Germany. After World War I, the German nation was devastated. The economy was in shambles, major banks were collapsing, and food riots were erupting in the streets. The economic chaos caused the spread of intense destabilization and social unrest. The German people were desperate and overwhelmed because their nation was on the verge of collapse.

Enter Adolf Hitler.

Hitler crafted a powerful and insidious narrative that he sold to the German people. He offered them a scapegoat for their problems and pains by placing responsibility at the feet of the Jews. Hitler's story about the Jews was simple and persuasive. In his dark narrative, the Jews were less than human. They were responsible for all of German society's ills, so they had to be eliminated. Hitler used the power of story to make the Jews an object of collective hatred. The Germans found solace in blaming their hopelessness, frustration, and anger on someone else.

Speaking of his mission to persuade the German people with his narrative about the Jews, Hitler wrote in *Mein Kampf,* "[F]rom the child's primer down to the last newspaper, every theater and every movie house, every advertising pillar and every billboard must be pressed into the service subjected of this one great mission. . . ."

Hitler believed that controlling the narrative was as important as controlling the military. One of his first leadership tactics was establishing the Ministry of Public Enlightenment and Propaganda and appointing Joseph Goebbels to direct it. Goebbels's strategy was guided by this philosophy: "Propaganda must prepare the way for practical actions. It must follow these actions step by step, never losing sight of them. . . . Such propaganda in the end miraculously makes the unpopular popular, enabling even a government's most difficult decisions to secure the resolute support of the people. A government that uses it properly can do what is necessary without the risk of losing the masses."[48]

Goebbels was directed to spread Hitler's dark narrative about the Jews to all of Germany. He penetrated virtually every sector of German society. The Nazi narrative about the Jews was repeated in every theater, on every radio station, on billboards and posters, at rallies, and even in children's schoolbooks. It didn't take long for the story to take root in the hearts and minds of the German people.

One by one, they were won over by a powerful narrative. A national culture of Nazism emerged, and 6 million people were heartlessly slaughtered—an entire race nearly extinguished from the face of the earth.

It is almost incomprehensible how so much devastation and death resulted from the spread of this wicked story. But such is the power of story. Stories can inspire us to rise and defend the weak, to sacrifice our lives for the cause of justice. Or they can inspire us to do unthinkable evil.

> A person captivated by porn's story can become trapped in that story because of its addictive qualities. Today, scores of us are getting stuck in the story of porn—a story that doesn't acknowledge values, human dignity, or the preservation of society.

During the time of the transatlantic slave trade, propaganda, in the form of story, was used to deceive the public into believing that slavery was a good institution, that slaves were content with their social status, and that slavery was necessary for economic prosperity.

In 1837 John Calhoun (a former Vice President of the United States) stood before the US Senate and boldly and passionately declared, "I hold [slavery] to be a positive good. . . . I appeal to facts. Never before has the black race of Central Africa, from the dawn of history to the present day, attained a condition so civilized and so improved, not only physically, but morally and intellectually."[49]

Thomas Dew, president of The College of William & Mary, argued that masters treated their slaves with "such benevolence and fairness that the slaves responded with joyful obedience." Dew added that the relation between master and slave resembled that of parent and child.[50]

In his 1855 book, *The Hireling and the Slave*, William John Grayson painted a rosy picture of what slavery was like, proclaiming, "Slavery ensures homes, food, and clothing for all. It permits no idleness, and it provides for sickness, infancy and old age."[51]

Clearly, <u>society believed the dominant narrative about slavery</u>, that it was a social good. People tolerated, welcomed, and perpetuated this harmful institution until the false story was finally replaced with truth by abolitionists in Great Britain and the United States. Only after the abolitionists began to tell a new story about slavery did public sentiment start to shift.

<u>Why do stories hold such power over us? First, let's consider</u> how a <u>story impacts the brain</u>. Our real-life experiences release certain chemicals in our brain, and the same thing happens when we experience a story. Famed American novelist George R.R. Martin observed, "A reader lives a thousand lives before he dies. . . . The man who never reads lives only one."[52] In other words, stories enable us to "live" things we might never experience in real life.

When you read about Middle Earth or watch onscreen as Frodo navigates the treacherous cliffs of Mount Doom, you feel that you are right there with him. You experience his adventure. Scientists call this type of <u>neural coupling "narrative transport" or "transportation theory."</u>[53]

When we listen to a riveting story or watch a captivating movie, the brain activates just as it would if we were in the middle of the drama ourselves. Did you choke up when the dying Johnny Cade told Ponyboy to "stay gold"? Thousands of others shared your emotions when they watched (or read) *The Outsiders*.[54] Enthralling stories have power over human minds. <u>We internalize stories. We experience them vicariously. They affect us profoundly.</u>

According to researchers, this transportation into a narrative world activates us cognitively, emotionally, and experientially. Research has also shown that there are profound (and often long-term) consequences of becoming immersed in a story. Immersion into a powerful narrative can inspire deep personal change, as we connect with a story and identify with its characters.[55]

The impact of stories on humans continues to attract the attention of researchers,[56] who note that when people lose themselves in a story, it changes their attitudes and intentions. This concept bears repeating: Engaging with a story is a transformative experience. That's why Plato, in outlining his perfect society, suggested that leaders control which stories the populace was allowed to read (or see performed). He understood the profound power of stories to define a culture, and he understood that storytellers possessed the ability to shape the way people thought about their world.[57]

Whoever Controls the Narrative Controls the Society

In previous generations, thought leaders revered and understood the power of stories. Parents, schoolteachers, community leaders, religious leaders, and village sages shared stories with the masses. Their stories did more than entertain; they instilled values, preserved the culture, built character, and gave people a sense of history—which helped them form their identities. That's why stories were crafted and chosen with great care.

Today, however, multi-billion-dollar media corporations have usurped the role of storytellers in society. The advertising industry, gaming industry, television industry, film industry, and music industry serve as our collective sages. These large, financially motivated corporations dominate communication in our world, and their priority isn't to build character, educate, or instill values. They seek to turn a profit at any cost. Cash is king, and the bottom line usually dictates which stories get told to the masses. The sacred role of storyteller has been sacrificed to the highest bidder, on the altar of capitalism.

In our visual age, media entrepreneurs have found a clever device to draw attention to their stories. Whether you are selling cologne, a car, or a song, mainstream media has discovered the power of incorporating explicit sexual imagery to lure people in: Miley Cyrus writhes naked on a wrecking ball and licks the tip of a hammer. Cardi B sings about her "WAP." Beyoncé works a stripper pole in the video "Partition."

Some readers may remember the famous Carl's Jr. Super Bowl ad, featuring Paris Hilton washing a car in a revealing swimsuit—while practically having sex with a hamburger. Sex has become a part of many of the stories we see today whether it makes logical sense or not.

Popular streaming sites make explicit sex a staple.

"Sex sells" isn't part of the American vernacular for nothing. Humans are driven by biological urges. Eating and mating are evolutionary necessities. We are biologically driven toward sex, and media moguls have no qualms about exploiting our sex drives to increase their profits.

Enter porn.

The porn industry has exploited human sexuality more than any other. If the pop-culture presentation of sexuality is a gateway drug, porn is like mainlining heroin. Far beyond the "softcore porn" of mainstream media, the porn industry tells the most potent story of all. Porn's portrayal of men, women, and sexuality is uniquely potent because it is hardwired into our bodies via arousal and orgasm. No other story evokes such a powerful physical and psychological response. Every pornographic image or scene presents a narrative of who men and women are, and how they should relate to one another. Consumers are conditioned to keep coming back for more.

As we will detail later in the book, a person captivated by porn's story can become trapped in that story because of its addictive qualities. Today, scores of us are getting stuck in the story of porn—a story that doesn't acknowledge values, human dignity, or the preservation of society.

Most American consumers are unaware that pornography is controlled by a handful of behemoth companies who rule the industry and control the stories of who we are and what sex is for. A few multi-billion-dollar porn "Walmarts" control tube sites, such as Xvideos.com, Pornhub.com, and Xnxx.com, which are colonizing the sexuality of a generation.

Why? Because they have gained control of the narrative about what it means to be a sexual being in today's world. And this potent narrative is being told to nearly every child growing up in our tech-saturated world.

There are serious implications for the stories a culture tells, especially to its children. That's why it's vital to understand the stories our children are growing up on and how those stories will shape their future. Stories affect and influence today's kids, and the tale of porn is certainly no exception. This story shapes our culture and changes our world.

The story of porn is making the unacceptable seem acceptable, just as it did during the rise of Nazi Germany and during the days of the slave trade.

3

PORN'S STORY ABOUT MEN

"The measure of a man is
what he does with power."

—PLATO

n the "Porn Universe," the Porn Man is single-minded, object-focused, sexually aggressive, shallow, narcissistic, and dominating. Above all, Porn Man uses his power to dominate the Porn Woman.

This dynamic takes many forms: student and teacher, father and daughter, doctor and patient, parent and babysitter, boyfriend and girlfriend, older brother and younger sister, etc. The scenarios vary, but the men are consistent in their use of physical power, social status, and wealth to subjugate women. (In rare cases, porn flips the script to make the woman the controller, but abuse of power is always wrong, no matter the gender of the abuser.)

At its core, porn is the story of exploiting power dynamics. It's a brand of sexuality that elevates one person while degrading the other.

In scene after scene, men exercise absolute power over women by humiliating, dominating, subjugating, and violating them sexually. One porn director told me (anonymously) that his goal was to get women naked and then punish them. Porn Man achieves that goal. He dehumanizes women, apparently unaware of the irony that he must dehumanize himself in the process.

The Porn Man Is Not Human

As we learned earlier, empathy is vital to ethical sexuality. But Porn Man is completely devoid of empathy, largely because he has been stripped of his humanity. Instead of a caring, thinking individual, he is like a beast without conscience, prowling for any female in heat so he can mount her. His advances aren't informed by any normal social cues—only by raw sexual aggression.

He sees a woman reading a book and he pounces. He enters a bedroom and sees a woman sleeping. He pulls out his penis and undresses the woman, who seems barely aware of what is happening to her.

Porn Man joins a babysitter on the couch and pulls her head into his lap.

Porn Man interrupts a woman doing yoga and rips her pants off from behind, without uttering a word.

Here is how Gail Dines, a sociologist and women's rights activist, describes Porn Man: "In pornography, men have no morality, they have no empathy, they have nothing. They are just a life support system for an erect penis."[58]

Yes, the men in porn seem incapable of connecting on a relationship level. They show no interest in a woman's well-being, feelings, or pleasure. They are devoid of compassion, emotional intelligence, sensitivity, or any core human quality. They are empty shells with one purpose: to get off. The way porn depicts men is sad. They are reduced to sex-crazed beasts who have no access to their emotions. They can't connect relationally with another human being. They can't show care, compassion, or (most importantly) empathy. In most mainstream porn, the man doesn't want to merely possess a woman; he wants to use her as a sexual object. There is no relational intimacy, no mutuality. Porn Man gets pleasure from using his power to subjugate and degrade women.

In the real world, someone who finds pleasure in causing another's pain enters the realm of diagnosable mental disorders—like sadism.

Often, someone whose brain is incapable of empathy is diagnosed as a psychopath. A recent University of Chicago study found that psychopaths' brains do not allow them to feel another's pain. Brain scans reveal that when these people imagine someone in pain, activity increases in the ventral striatum, the part of the brain that helps to produce feelings of pleasure.[59] By all definitions, Porn Man is a sadistic psychopath.

The Porn Man's Body Is a Weapon

Porn Man's lack of empathy and his thirst for absolute power are evident across the spectrum of pornography. Sometimes he is dehumanizing, animalistic, and narcissistic, using women as objects. Other times he is sadistically malevolent. His phallus is a weapon intended to inflict pain on women so that he can feel powerful.

Pornography disregards women's humanity; it does the same thing to men. The penis, a body part designed to provide an intimate physical connection and help to create life, becomes a fearful weapon, intended to intimidate, abuse, humiliate, and degrade.

In porn, an abnormally large penis is usually the only male body part that is brought into sharp focus or seen in a close-up. Marketing messages consistently eroticize the way a man's penis will be used to harm and dominate a woman.

A staple of pornography is the scene in which a man (or group of men) uses the penis to gag a woman, stretch her anus, "pound" her vagina, slap her face, or otherwise "punish" or "destroy" her. Such words are popular when porn marketers describe their brand of entertainment.

Inflicting pain and injury is particularly popular in interracial porn. Many of these productions feature large Black men aggressively penetrating small-framed white women. This racist sub-genre has skyrocketed in popularity. Productions like *Blacked: Interracial Icon 10* are typically among AVN's "most downloaded" videos worldwide. In the aforementioned film, a petite white woman is accosted by seven towering Black men who simultaneously (and violently) penetrate her every orifice, stretching them until she is wincing, cringing, and screaming.

Such behavior isn't reserved for interracial porn, however. "Punishing" a woman with a weaponized penis is a staple of almost all types of pornography. A quick search on Pornhub reveals this eroticized destruction of women in a seemingly endless number of violent titles, such as *Tushy: Punished Teen Gets Sodomized!* (which had more than 12 million views when this chapter was written). *Slutty Latina Gets Destroyed* had collected more than 14 million views, while *White Whore Destruction 2* had amassed more than 6 million.

Porn Man's body is deployed to test a woman's pain threshold: physically, mentally, emotionally, and psychologically. How far can he push a woman before he breaks her—before she is so humiliated and degraded that she is left crying in agony? Before she is bruised and has suffered injuries to her anus or vagina.

One well-known porn producer told me this about the scenes he creates: "It's a great experience to find out what the limit is—you push to the limit to find out... how much can she take before she stops and says, 'Oh my god, I can't take it anymore,' you know?"

He smiled eerily at me as he confessed, "And that happens all the time. . . because the stuff that we're doing is not normal at all, not normal sex."

He added, "I mean, we're working brand-new girls, so they've never been just hammered and tossed around like a rag doll. . . . There have been a few meltdowns on the set, and we kept the camera rolling."[60] What this man described to me is not unique to his films. He represents what is now common in mainstream porn—the absolute degradation of women in the most painful ways possible.

As Porn Man progresses down the rabbit hole of what is possible when absolute power and the lack of empathy fuse, the malevolent nature of his sexuality results in the sexual torture of women. The popularity of BDSM (bondage and discipline, dominance and submission, and sadomasochism and masochism) videos reveals that people want to see women suffer. That is the purpose of sexual interactions for too many people.

It's deeply concerning how many men buy into porn's perspective on power. They seem to enjoy watching an avatar use his physical, social, and economic power to subjugate, humiliate, and ultimately destroy women. This is porn's story about men.

One of Pornhub's most popular videos (with millions of views) depicts a "teen" with hands and feet shackled to the floor. Her mouth is gagged, and she is penetrated by a machine, electrocuted, and burned with candle wax.[61] In this video, like so many others, a woman's humanity is portrayed only so that it can be destroyed later, destroyed in a way that arouses the viewer.

One popular porn producer told me (anonymously) that he hasn't reached satisfaction in his scenes until "she is in a heap on the floor," a scenario he describes as "the most beautiful thing in the world." Another producer conceded to me that after one of his scenes, the female performer ended up in the corner of a room, sucking her thumb in the fetal position, because she was so devastated by what had happened to her.[62] This is porn's culmination of male power: a woman in a heap on the floor, devastated and destroyed.

The Porn Man's Appeal to Male Consumers

One may cringe at the thought of masses of men staring at their smartphones, hands in their pants, and experiencing sexual pleasure as they watch women being destroyed. Sadly, this is what happens—millions of times a day on Pornhub alone (130 million times per day, to be exact.)

Surely, not all porn viewers are sadists, so what attracts them? What makes this cocktail of sex and domination so enticing and intoxicating?

First, we humans have the desire for power and sex built into our nature. Psychologists and sociologists have identified the "need for power"—the desire to influence the world around us—as an unconscious motivator of human behavior. Indeed, the longing for power is as old as humankind itself. In 1933, psychologist Henry Murray recognized it as one of our basic human needs.[63] We want to make our mark on the world and exercise influence over our circumstances and surroundings.

Pornographers have astutely identified the existential human longing for power and sex and have capitalized by crafting their stories to keep consumers coming back for more.

The visceral nature of pornography bypasses our critical thinking capacities and appeals to the "reptilian brain." Pornographers intentionally create a transporting story for viewers, giving them the simulated experience of achieving sexual power in a way they don't experience in real life. Pornographers create a total mind and body experience for the consumer.

One pornographer I interviewed explained how he intentionally films his scenes so that the male consumer can vicariously insert himself into the stories. He instructs the women in his scenes to call the men "mister" instead of using a real name. Thus, any male viewer could be her virtual partner. He also directs women to address the camera so that the male viewer can easily imagine interacting with them.

Porn's male-dominated scenarios allow viewers to enter the sexual utopia of the Porn Universe. Porn Man is their avatar as he experiences absolute sexual power—something that does not exist for men in the "real world." One porn actor told me:

> I mean, it's the power struggle, isn't it? We all wish we were more powerful. We wish we were the head of states or, you know, big important people in society. Falling short of that, you can get some of that on a one-to-one basis by overpowering another person . . . in a sexual manner.
>
> You know, you're the big alpha male and she's the little dependent female who's now being overpowered. It's tough to say because I guess it's almost dark enough that I don't wanna analyze it. I just wanna enjoy it . . . because if I start thinking about it too much, the magic may disappear, and I may not enjoy it anymore.[64]

It's not hard to understand the appeal of porn's alpha-male world. One man wants to be a CEO, but he is stuck in an hourly job. Another wants to be a major social-media influencer, but he lives in relative anonymity. He wants to sleep with an attractive woman in his apartment complex, but she has rejected him repeatedly. A teen lusts after a cheerleader, but she won't give him the time of day.

Guys like this can be vicariously satiated through porn. After all, Porn Man is never rejected, never told no. (Yes, some porn scenarios involve a woman saying no—but her refusal is overpowered by emotional manipulation or brute physical force. And in pornography, unlike the real world, there are no consequences for violating a woman's boundaries.)

Additionally, Porn Man takes no social risks, invests nothing emotionally. He assumes no responsibility in his "relationships." Despite his loathsome behavior, he maintains all the power and engages in any form of sex he desires.

Of course, porn's portrayal of power imbalances and sex with no social costs appeals to incels (males who are involuntarily celibate), but it also engages married men or single men who date regularly. Some male celebrities, including A-list actors and superstar athletes (who have sexual access to many women), admit to regular porn use. Even the rich and powerful can't resist the allure of exercising power over a woman and dominating her sexually, regardless of her preferences, feelings, or consent. And it's all just a click away.

It's deeply concerning how many men buy into porn's perspective on power. They seem to enjoy watching an avatar use his physical, social, and economic power to subjugate, humiliate, and ultimately destroy women. This is porn's story about men—about who they are, what their purpose is, and how they should behave with women. Today's males experience this story with frightening frequency, at progressively younger ages. Porn's story is one of the most destructive forces ever introduced into society, and it's devastating men, women, kids, and teens.

Now that we have explored porn's story about men, it's time to focus on its story about women.

4

PORN'S STORY ABOUT WOMEN

*"The human species thinks in metaphors
and learns through stories."*

—MARY CATHERINE BATESON[65]

L
ike the Porn Man, the Porn Woman plays a consistent role. In reality, women are complex, multifaceted, deep, and autonomous beings who have histories, memories, feelings, preferences, and agency—along with everything else that makes them uniquely and wonderfully human.

Porn tells a different story. In the Porn Universe, Porn Woman is hollow, artificial, and one-dimensional. Porn's view of women is conveyed in word and deed, and the picture it paints profoundly affects us all, as individuals and as a society.

Pornography indoctrinates viewers through immersion, arousal, and orgasm. As noted earlier, consumers internalize its message because porn is a mind-and-body experience. It is the most powerful form of propaganda on the planet. And porn's propaganda about who women are and how they should be treated is influencing the psyches of us all, but especially those who are coming of age in our digital world. Let's examine the story of Porn Woman in detail.

If you were to explore today's internet porn sites, you would find scores of different scenarios, united by a common theme: Girl calls plumber to fix a leaky faucet and sex ensues. Girl calls pizza delivery man and sex ensues. Girl goes to tutor after school and sex ensues. Girl shows up to babysit and sex ensues. Girl is picked up on the side of the road and sex ensues. Secretary stays late at work and has sex with her boss. Burglar breaks into a home and has sex with his victim. Cheerleader has sex with the football coach. Brother has sex with his sister. Mom has sex with her son. Dad has sex with his daughter—and sometimes Mom joins in. Mom has sex with her son and daughter. The variations on the theme seem endless, but the narrative about women is consistent: They are not viewed as human. They are sex objects.

The Porn Woman Is Not Human

The Porn Woman is, first and foremost, the sexual property of men. She exists to be Porn Man's masturbatory aid. None of porn's boundless scenarios acknowledge her humanity. Porn Woman is degraded, humiliated, aggressively penetrated, and abused. She is stripped of her agency and dehumanized.

Some porn productions feature only one form of exploitation; others feature a variety. But in all mainstream porn, Porn Woman is forced to welcome and enjoy her abuse—then beg for more. Through it all, she must ensure the viewer that she "deserves" what is being done to her. Her forced smile says, "I accept my place in this world, and I welcome my relegation to a subhuman class."

Pornographers employ several tactics to degrade women and portray them as less than human. For example, women in porn are called "bitches," "cum dumpsters," "sluts," and "whores." She is not Sarah; she is a "bitch"—a female dog.

She is not a person who has worth; she is a "cum dumpster"—a trash receptacle for men's ejaculate. She is not an equal member of society who deserves respect; she is a "slut"—a name used to shame and silence her.

The words spoken to Porn Woman never affirm her humanity. No one sincerely asks about her pleasure or well-being. In porn, dialogue is sparse, but when words are spoken, they are used to convey contempt to women.

As harmful as the words are, porn's actions truly make their mark on Porn Woman's body.

The most obvious and ubiquitous action that demonstrates Porn Woman's worth is the Porn Man's ejaculation. In porn, a man uses his semen to "mark" a woman as his property and to show his disdain for her. In most scenes, he accomplishes this by ejaculating on her face, in what is called "the money shot," "cum shot," or "pop shot."

Porn Man will cover her eyes, nose, mouth, and hair with his semen. Porn Woman often flinches as she awaits her humiliation, but she does her best to maintain a fake smile. The scene recalls a dog lifting his leg to urinate on a tree to claim it as his territory, his property.

The Porn Woman is also degraded by being commanded to swallow semen. Men in the porn industry have expressed disgust at the idea of ingesting semen, yet it is something the Porn Woman is required to do, fake-moaning with pleasure.

Bill Margold, a well-known porn performer and industry spokesperson, revealed that he once ingested his own semen (from a woman's body) during a sex scene. Other males on the set expressed disgust at him. He confessed, "The men on the set said things like, 'That's the most disgusting thing I've ever seen.' When I bring it up today, men get queasy...."[66]

The double standard is obvious. Something that is "beneath" a male performer is definitely not beneath a woman. In porn, nothing is beneath a woman. Porn Woman has almost no value.

Finally, male ejaculation serves as a punctuation mark, signifying Porn Woman's lack of worth. It's a visible sign that Porn Man is finished with her. The visibility of Porn Man's ejaculate in virtually every porn scene is the required proof that he has experienced his pleasure. No such evidence of her pleasure is needed. Porn Woman is merely an object that he uses to get himself off. She is not a human with preferences, emotions, agency, or desires of her own. Her pleasure and happiness have no meaning. The best she can do is affirm her own degradation. She is not a whole human being, but merely a body with various holes that must be penetrated with as much force as possible.

This degradation is even worse in "gangbang porn." According to a UCLA study, more than 42 percent of porn performers have engaged in this act.[67] In most gangbang porn, a group of men add insult to injury by ending an aggressive sex scene with "bukkake," ejaculating on their victim's face and body.

Often, this female is visibly disgusted. She gags as she attempts to wipe the fluid from her eyes and spit it out of her mouth. But through it all, she tries to give the camera the impression that she is enjoying herself. Through words and actions, porn presents women as sub-human objects. Just like the meat at your local grocery store, women are sold piece by piece. The camera focuses on tight shots of their breasts, vaginas, anuses, and mouths.

Only in porn do viewers witness an entire screen being filled with an anus being stretched by an abnormally large penis (sometimes two of them). Other extreme close-ups focus on a woman's breasts as they are manipulated aggressively, or her vagina being "pounded" with relentless force. When her face is shown, it's only to reinforce the message that she is okay with what is happening to her. Her eyes reveal her pain, but her game smile tries to convince the viewer that she is enjoying her humiliation and destruction.

Porn objectifies a woman's body, part by part. She is judged on the tidiness of her pubic hair, the symmetry of her labia, and the size of her areolae. Even the color of her anal sphincter is up for judgment.

The standards vary, according to the type of pornography. In "barely legal" porn, the woman's breasts must appear underdeveloped, creating the fantasy that she is very young. Her frame should be small, without too many curves. In MILF* porn, however, her breasts must be large. In porn that features anal sex, women are expected to have bleached anuses.

In nearly all porn, women are expected to have minimal body fat and hairless (or nearly hairless) vaginas. But pornography takes a woman's dehumanization even further. Porn Woman is frequently reduced to animal status. (It should be noted, however, that PETA would protest if animals were treated like porn actresses.)

The film *Fucked Like an Animal* (produced by a company called Sexually Broken) has received millions of views on Pornhub. This film, part of the "Treat Her Like a Lady" series, features women in dog collars being assaulted in various ways. Their hands are bound as they are choked, struck, and violently penetrated.

This hate-filled series has a clear theme: Treating a woman "like a lady" means degrading, humiliating, and abusing her.

The animalization of women in porn goes beyond the name-calling described earlier. Consider how we speak to our dogs. We don't ask them to do things; we command them. We are their masters, and they are required to obey us when we order them to sit, stay, lie down, or roll over. Women in porn are commanded similarly. They are not addressed as human beings. They are commanded to "shut up," "suck harder," "open wider," and "swallow."

---

* MILF stands for "Mother I'd Like to Fuck"

41

Let's consider this aspect of porn's story: Men give the commands; women are expected to obey them. Agency has no place in the interaction. A woman's freedom and preferences are unimportant. As the various scenarios unfold, Porn Woman is expected to obey commands, just like a well-trained dog.

Pornography eroticizes domination in an effort to arouse the viewer. As we learned in the previous chapter, the story of porn is a story of power—men's power to dominate and control women like they are animals. This power imbalance is no accident. It's organic to almost every porn script.

Porn's narrative about women is carefully calculated by writers, directors, and producers. It makes a clear, existential statement about who women are—something less than human.

In a speech titled "Pornography Happens to Women," author and activist Andrea Dworkin explained:

> When we talk about pornography that objectifies women, we are talking about the sexualization of insult, of humiliation. . . . We are also talking about the sexualization of cruelty. And I want to say to you—there is cruelty that does not have in it overt violence. . . . There is cruelty that says "you are worth nothing in human terms" . . . that says "you exist in order for him to ejaculate on you; that's who you are, that's what you are for." Dehumanizing someone is cruel, and it does not have to be violent in order for it to be cruel.[68]

Cruelty toward women, in one form or another, dominates mainstream porn today. Physical violence toward women is a staple, of course. However, as Dworkin notes, porn doesn't have to be overtly violent to be degrading, humiliating, and cruel. There are other ways to punish and dehumanize Porn Woman, simply for being a woman.

Porn Woman Must Be Subjected to Sexual Violence

Whether it is the pizza delivery guy, the yoga instructor, the professor, or the plumber, you can almost certainly expect that what you are going to see in porn is some combination of aggressive sexual behavior.

In fact, a 2020 study of 4,009 heterosexual scenes from two major tube sites (Pornhub and Xvideos) revealed that 45 percent of the Pornhub scenes and 35 percent of the Xvideos scenes featured at least one act of aggression toward women (including choking, slapping, biting, punching, and bondage).[69] Another study (published in 2018) examined 172 popular heterosexual porn films from Pornhub and found that nearly 60 percent of them showed physical aggression or verbal aggression toward women by men. (The study excluded group sex scenes, which are often some of the most aggressive.) Researcher Dr. Eran Shor concluded that "a considerable portion of popular pornographic videos . . . legitimate and even celebrate aggression and degradation."[70] The bottom line: Aggressive, "hardcore" sexual encounters dominate today's online porn menu.

Tanya, a former porn performer I interviewed, described being part of an industry that turns violence against women into sexual entertainment. Tanya is a beautiful young woman with a small frame. As she sat in front of me, bravely recalling her years in the porn industry, her voice cracked, her lip quivered, and tears pooled in her eyes.

Like many women in porn, Tanya entered the industry when her family experienced financial hardship. Her roommate at the time was in porn and suggested that Tanya try it, which she did. However, she had no idea what she was getting into, or the toll it would take on her: physically, mentally, and emotionally.

Tanya became tense as she described her first experience in porn: "The sex, I thought it would be normal, like what I was used to in a relationship. [But] then I get there and I'm getting hit, and beat-up, and ripped. I'm in pain to where I'm screaming. I was screaming so bad because it was so painful, and I was ripped. I was in bed for three days after that scene, because I couldn't move."

Unfortunately, painful, violent sex became Tanya's norm. "Ninety-eight percent of the scenes that I did were extremely rough," she told me. "It was violent. And it was point-blank to show throwing up, gagging, crying—that's what they're there to show."[71]

Some readers might wonder why Tanya returned to filming after that horrific first day. First, like many women in porn, she found herself far from home, living in a strange place with a group of women who were all strangers to her. And she had no transportation, other than a driver who took her to and from filming locations. She felt isolated from anything normal, trapped in porn's story, just like the characters she portrayed. Abuse, degradation, and hopelessness became her cultural reality.

Indeed, Porn Woman is expected to tolerate aggressive and violent sex acts. They are the norm in mainstream porn. Peer-reviewed research demonstrates that violence in porn is not relegated to the darkest corners of the industry. Violent porn is consistently ranked as some of the most popular content on the world's most-trafficked sites.

A 2020 study of 4,009 heterosexual scenes from two major tube sites (Pornhub and Xvideos) revealed that 45 percent of the Pornhub scenes and 35 percent of the Xvideos scenes featured at least one act of aggression toward women (including choking, slapping, biting, punching, and bondage).

In any other context, such violence toward women would evoke protest. After all, our natural reaction to violence is to recoil, defend ourselves, or avoid it all costs. Even animals have the sense to run from violence. Porn Woman, however, is different. She submits to violence, and in some cases even appears to enjoy it.

The Porn Woman Submits to, Enjoys, Desires, and Deserves Her Treatment

In the Porn Universe, women are expected to submit to sexual domination and aggression. As we learned earlier in this chapter, Porn Woman is often judged on how well she can take pain, how much ejaculate she can swallow. Consider *The Gangbang of Riley Reid*, one of the most-downloaded videos in recent years. The film's official synopsis describes Riley being "put to the test" by having extremely rough sex with 26 men.

The synopsis adds, "The spinner [porn slang for a very petite woman with a small frame] is tried and tested as the men pass her around and sample her . . . and even manage to stuff her booty with double anal!" (Two penises in one anus.)

Here's the concluding line: "Watch the adorable Riley Reid like you have never seen her before in two of the most amazing gangbangs you will ever witness! Will her holes ever recover?"[72] Films like this portray the myth that a woman is attractive, even "adorable" because her child-like body can withstand aggressive penetration and ejaculation from dozens of men, in every orifice, and with a smile on her face. She is valued for being the willing and submissive recipient of male aggression and disdain.

One porn producer explained it to me this way: "Jamie Lynn Heart? She was great. . . . She was the perfect victim. She was whimpering and crying and getting into it . . . whimpering, crying, and loving it. She ended it [her scene] with this brilliant smile, looking right at the camera . . . her face was all fucked up—saying, 'I hope you liked me, Mister.'"[73]

Scenes like these are common. In early 2020, one of Pornhub's most-watched videos (with more than 5 million views) was a film called *No Mercy Anal Compilation: Tight Teens Relentless Rough Fucking Painal.* The film features notorious porn performer James Deen, who has been accused of rape and assault by several women. In the film, Deen strangles, hits, and spits on the women. He pins their faces to the floor while violently and painfully penetrating them anally—what the porn industry calls "painal."[74]

The women wince, cringe, and scream in pain, but they also smile and moan while their anuses are stretched so far and pounded so hard that they become red, raw, and "gaping." This painful injury done to women in porn is taken to the extreme in what the industry calls "rosebudding." Painful anal penetration causes a woman to suffer rectal prolapse. The walls of her rectum (which is the last section of the large intestine) drop out of her anus. Even in this gruesome scenario, a woman experiencing what a doctor might call a serious bodily injury does so with a smile and a moan of pleasure.

The scenes described above are not exceptions. In the previously mentioned study of popular mainstream porn films, researchers found that in almost 90 percent of the scenes in which women were being choked, gagged, bitten, punched, kicked, shoved, confined, bound, and mutilated, they responded with "moans of pleasure" or displayed no visible reaction at all.[75]

This unnatural response to degradation and pain sends a potent message: Women enjoy degrading and violent sex. At the very least, they don't mind it. The ideal Porn Woman is, to borrow the phrasing of a popular 2018 video, "a true pain slut."[76]

In porn, women consistently validate and reinforce the weaponization of male sexuality. They confirm its acceptability by being unfailingly receptive and responsive to hyper-aggressive and violent men. Every sexual advance, no matter how ferocious, is readily accepted by Porn Woman. The more aggressive the advance, the more pleasurable the sex appears to be for her.

And that's not the end of the story. Porn Woman doesn't merely enjoy being objectified and subjected to degrading sex; she hunts for it. Women in porn are depicted as sex-obsessed. They are hypersexual, sex-starved, and voracious sex-bots. They need sex like they need air and water. And they seem to have no interests beyond sex. Porn Woman eagerly spreads her legs and opens her mouth for any penis, regardless of whom it is attached to or how painfully it is inserted.

A popular myth, especially among men, is that victims of sexual assault deserve it, perhaps even desire it. We've all heard the adage, "She got what she wanted."

Somehow, women who are sexually harassed or assaulted "asked for it." Porn's typical story lines reinforce this myth. The viewer is absolved of any moral conflict over the degrading and humiliating treatment he is witnessing.

A woman's anus becomes raw, swollen, or even torn from violent penetration. She vomits after being gagged by multiple penises. Her face grows red and bruised from being slapped and punched. Her mascara runs as she cries out in pain and humiliation. But she "deserves" it all. The viewers at home feel no guilt. They wash their hands of any culpability. After all, "The whore got what she deserved."

Porn Woman's Vulnerabilities Exist to Be Exploited

Women in porn are often portrayed as defenseless and powerless. They are easily coerced or manipulated. These vulnerabilities are exploited and eroticized as women become the targets of male aggressors.

Another popular Pornhub video, *Little Asian Step-sis Gets Stuck and Fucked*, features "stuck porn." The video begins with a young, small-framed woman attempting to fix a leaky pipe under the kitchen sink. Her wrists become trapped, so that her torso is inside the cabinet while her lower half is exposed outside. The video's director devotes plenty of footage to the woman's struggles to free herself, so that the viewer is convinced that she is indeed trapped. Exhausted, she finally gives up and wonders aloud when her stepbrother will return to free her. On cue, the older brother enters the kitchen and assesses the situation. Then, instead of helping his sister, he takes advantage of her, despite her protests. After molesting her with his hands, he unzips his pants and aggressively rapes her anally and vaginally. The camera shows close-ups of the woman's face as she grimaces and screams.

The brother ends the scene by ejaculating on his sister's buttocks, then leaving her, stuck and humiliated.[77]

This video, and millions like it, underscore a woman's place and purpose to the viewer. She is prey; men are the predators. Her vulnerabilities are not to be protected; they should be exploited, in the most aggressive way possible, for male sexual gratification.

Porn actress Cameron Bay tearfully described to me her degrading experience in porn. (She left the industry after contracting HIV/AIDS, most likely while filming a violent scene.) But before hearing the story from Bay herself, consider the marketing copy for her film:

"Cameron Bay loves attention, but she has no idea what she's in for when she signs up for Public Disgrace. Lorelei . . . drags her into a dirty club where Cameron immediately has her clothes ripped off by the rough crowd. She [is] called names by strangers, bent over a table [to receive anal penetration]. . . . But the biggest humiliation . . . comes when Cameron is made to stand alone on stage and foolishly attempt to masturbate with her bound hands. When she can't . . . a team . . . pins her down. . . . When she is utterly destroyed . . . Cameron is tied to a stairway and made to take the cattle prod. Finished with this slut, Lorelei leaves her tied there, a plaything for the lustful bar patrons."

Bay is a young woman with soulful eyes and a gentle voice. In her interview for this book, she described how she truly felt about the scene described above: "It's crazy because when people sit and watch this for entertainment, they don't realize the mindset that you have to have in order to do this. It's scary; it's very scary, 'cause you just blank it out. I don't really remember much of anything. I just remember starting; I remember stopping. . . . It felt like an out-of-body experience, and that's what's so scary about it, because I can't take it back. . . . That wasn't what I had signed up for. I [had to dissociate]; I mean, with what was going on, you kinda have to. For any person doing porn, you have to shut off your emotions, 'cause you can't get too emotionally involved. . . . I guess I just turned it off a little too much. Instead of dimming the lights, I just blacked out."

She added, "I don't believe in regretting things, but I have one regret, and that's not putting my foot down and protecting myself. . . . There was nobody to stop it from happening. I was tied up, so I couldn't stop it from happening."

At this point in the interview, tears were streaming down Bay's face. "I was a product," she said.[78] Indeed, Bay and other women in porn are not only reduced to animal status; they are regarded as mere products. They are inanimate objects, devoid of human dignity. They are routinely violated, degraded, and humiliated for the purpose of entertainment.

In February 2018, one of AVN's most-watched and most-rented videos for the month was titled *Tattooed Anal Sluts*. The marketing copy describes the women in the film as liking "extra rough" anal sex. The film synopsis says one of the women featured "gets tossed around and choked" while her anus "is punished" and her face is "covered in semen." Another woman is "spit on" and is aggressively penetrated but "still wears a smile."

If you think that these examples are extreme, think again. These are common scenarios in mainstream online porn today, and the faked "pleasure response" to degradation and pain sends a potent message: Women enjoy degrading and violent sex. Porn Woman consistently validates and reinforces the weaponization of male sexuality. She confirms its acceptability.

But What About Feminist Porn?

Pro-porn apologists cite "feminist" porn as an ethically sanitary and acceptable alternative to mainstream hardcore porn. However, even this fringe genre is rife with toxic messages about who women are and the place they occupy in the world. In many ways, feminist porn reinforces the larger narrative of mainstream porn.

For example, Erika Lust is a "feminist pornographer" who claims to create "ethical" porn. Lust, who is featured in Rashida Jones's Netflix documentary *Hot Girls Wanted: Turned On*, asserts in the series' first episode, "We don't want to get women out of porn; we want to get them into porn." Filmmakers like Lust claim that if women are behind the camera, the scenes will feature romance and sex that is enjoyed by the performers and appreciated by women watching.

The first episode of the series begins with scenes of flowers blowing in the wind, the sun shining, and horses frolicking on a farm. We hear soft music and the peaceful sounds of birds chirping in the background. Next, we are introduced to Holly, a porn photographer whose claim to fame is (according to her), creating "glamorous, beautiful" pornographic images. The story of Holly's life and the life of her mother, who is also a pornographer, are presented in a nostalgic and romantic way.

At one point, Holly proudly reminisces about a time her mother shot an eight-woman orgy for *Playboy* magazine. At this point, some viewers might be convinced that porn can be a healthy and happy place for women.

Eventually, viewers are transported to a feminist porn set, where Erika Lust works her magic. A young woman named Monica is seated at a piano and is about to embark on her first porn scene. She is wide-eyed and visibly nervous. The script says that she is going to act out her wildest fantasy of engaging in sex while she plays the piano on a stage. She anxiously fumbles through her lines a few times, as Erika grows impatient.

Then the male character appears and the sexual scene begins. During the scene, Monica is aggressively pummeled by the man from behind. Her hair is yanked back, and she is obviously in distress.

She pleads, "Stop! Please give me a moment; I need a moment."

Annoyed, someone in the crew asks why. Monica winces and explains, "I'm in pain."

But waiting will cost too much money. Everyone is on the clock. Erika, the "feminist hero" of this episode, orders Monica to "fake it." So much for "real female pleasure."

Trying to explain what has just transpired, Erika says, "Well, in the end, this is a film, and it is an illusion. I create the image that I want you to see as an audience."

The facade continues to fade when one investigates Lust's website and learns that her latest production features the mutilation, rape, and torture of a woman "submissive" by a man. Lust calls it "feminist submissive porn." If you are wondering how a man's rape and mutilation of a woman represents feminist ideals, you are not the only one.

In truth, feminist porn is no different than mainstream hardcore porn. Only the budget and the production values are higher.

Calling porn "feminist" or "empowering" doesn't change its basic nature. Porn's story about women is inherently objectifying, dehumanizing, and degrading. It's a misogynistic and dishonest story about who women are.

Porn Woman is consistently stripped of her humanity and served up as an object of male contempt and exploitation.

How Female Consumers Internalize the Porn Woman

Just as the Porn Man is used as an avatar who allows the male consumer to navigate the Porn Universe, female consumers navigate this world vicariously through the experience of the Porn Woman. The female porn consumer who begins her journey into porn at a young age (as most do) internalizes the role of Porn Woman. All of the domination, dehumanization, violence, and degradation become part of her sexual template.

She is conditioned to welcome aggression and abuse as erotic advances—to be met with enjoyment and sexual arousal. This point was driven home during my interview with famous porn producer Max Hardcore, when our microphones caught him (off camera) discussing his "craft" with porn performer Eric Swiss. "What people need to know," Hardcore said, "is that women are just meat muppets that need to be destroyed."[79]

We'll explore this conformity to Porn Woman in future chapters, but it's worth noting here that modern pornography's violations of a woman's physical, mental, emotional, and psychological integrity would have been unthinkable only a few years ago. The implications for young females growing up in the digital age are frightening.

5

GROWING UP ON THE STORY OF PORN

*"I remember having sex education class when I was in sixth grade,
twelve years old . . . which was almost comical because by that point
I had already seen, read, and experienced a lot from pornography . . .
it was ninety-five percent of my learning experience about sex."*

—TIM A., porn consumer [80]

welve-year-old Ethan is playing during recess with his best
friend, Daniel. Daniel tells Ethan that he's discovered a secret
video on his dad's laptop. For the first time in his life, he's seen
people having sex.

The boys rush to the restroom, and Daniel pulls out his iPhone.
Wide-eyed, they laugh nervously as Daniel types the word "sex
videos" into the search engine. Before they can click on the links,
however, someone opens the door, and they quickly hide the phone.
Recess is over.

After school, Ethan remains curious. He enters his room and
closes the door. On his tablet, he begins a Google search. Soon, he
discovers a variety of tube sites offering "millions of free videos."

A few clicks later, he's uncovered hundreds of graphic thumbnails. He can't believe his eyes. He reads the words, "Stepbrother, stepsister, itty bitty pussy, it's my turn, little sister."[81] That's weird, he thinks. He scrolls over the thumbnail and gasps in shock when the image comes to life.

Ethan sees a young-looking girl wearing a worried expression as her "brother" caresses her thigh. The film quickly cuts to a close-up of her being aggressively pounded vaginally, then cuts back to her face, which reveals discomfort and distress.

Ethan moves to the next title, *Tiny Teen Janice Gets Her Big Dick Wish Granted*.[82] As he hovers over the image, a preview shows a man grabbing a "teenage" girl by the hair and pressing her face into a mattress. She is clearly in pain. The camera pulls back to show the man forcefully penetrating her in the anus with his unnaturally large penis. Cut to the girl's face, grimacing in pain.

Ethan winces. He is frightened but intrigued. He feels shame flood through him as he scrolls over the next video, then the next. Why is his body responding so strangely? He is confused, but his heart is pounding like it did when he rode a roller coaster for the first time. He doesn't want to stop searching. He hears footsteps in the hallway and quickly closes the browser. He pulls up *Angry Birds* just before his mom opens the door. He has avoided getting caught, but a new world has opened to him: the vast universe of porn.

He doesn't realize it, but his understanding of sex has changed forever. The next afternoon, his curiosity gets the best of him again. He's back on the porn tube sites. Rinse and repeat . . . for the rest of his life.

Fifty years ago, before the explosion of the digital media age, a child's innocence endured as long as childhood itself. But in today's media-saturated world, too many kids are robbed of their innocence via the invasion of sexually graphic content. And it's happening under the noses of parents and other adult guardians. Believe it or not, the modern child is being raised on the story of porn. Kids in Spider-Man footie pajamas are browsing the web with ease and being exposed to pornography at ever-younger ages.

For example, a 2017 American Psychological Association (APA) study revealed that the average age of a male's first exposure to pornography is 13, with the earliest exposure as early as age 5.[83]

A 2019 research project commissioned by the British Board of Film Classification (BBFC) found that more than half (51 percent) of 11- to 13-year-olds reported having seen pornography. That viewing percentage rose to 66 percent of teens ages 14 to 15.[84]

Porn producers and performers are well aware of this trend. Nina Hartley, a well-known performer and outspoken advocate for the industry, admitted to me, "I have a family member who told me he discovered porn online at age nine. . . . And he was a gateway person [for his friends to be exposed to porn]."[85]

It's a sad irony that the more tech-savvy our kids become, the earlier they are exposed to porn.[86] Accessibility to porn is unfettered and unhindered for most children today. It's no shock that mobile devices are the primary means of porn exposure for children.[87] Based on a sample of 2,600 American tweens and teens, 53 percent of kids ages 8 to 12 own a tablet. Sixty-seven percent of teens own a smartphone.[88]

And, of course, even if a kid doesn't own a smartphone or tablet yet, most of his friends do. With such easy access to tech, it should surprise no one that our kids are spending a mind-bending amount of time looking at screens. According to a 2019 nationwide survey conducted by Common Sense Media, kids ages 8 to 12 spend almost five hours a day consuming "entertainment screen media." That number balloons to seven hours and 22 minutes for teens. And those totals don't include using a screen for homework or other school-related projects.[89]

Today it's as common to see a kid tapping away on a smartphone as it used to be to see a kid playing with Hot Wheels cars or a yo-yo. Because of this early exposure, porn is often a child's first interaction with human sexuality—an interaction with long-term implications, given the lack of input from traditional sources.

For example, there is little mentoring into a healthy sexuality from parents and others who can impart wisdom about what it means to be a man, a woman, and a sexual being in the world. In today's Western culture, the traditional ritual of initiation into adulthood is practically nonexistent.

What about sex education in our schools? According to the Scholars Strategy Network (scholars.org), only 38 percent of US high schools and 14 percent of middle schools provide comprehensive sex education—by teaching all nineteen of the sexual health topics considered essential by the Centers for Disease Control.[90] These topics include how to create and maintain a healthy and respectful relationship, preventing sexually transmitted diseases, and preventing pregnancy.

Thus, adolescents struggle to find answers to their questions about human sexuality. Porn has filled this vacuum. It's the primary source of "sex ed" for many of today's youth. It is initiating an entire generation of boys and girls into a deformed sexuality.

Male Sexual Initiation

Throughout history, coming-of-age rituals have been a fundamental part of human existence. These rituals often included the collective wisdom of the community being passed on to those crossing the threshold from childhood into adulthood. Young men learned how to understand their place in the world, how to establish an identity, and how to embrace the values that help them navigate the treacherous journey of life.

The rituals provided a firm foundation and endowed generation after generation with the tools necessary to function as adults. They provided the structure and stability needed to survive in an unpredictable and harsh world.

Young men learned, among other things, how to be responsible and respectful with their sexuality. They learned how to behave within their own families and within society at large.

Today, unfortunately, the initiation process has been hijacked by widespread exposure to porn's hardcore and deviant brand of sexuality.

Imagine a young teen boy, sitting alone and observing scene after scene of empty, aggressive sex. He is confused, embarrassed, and aroused—often all at once. He is in the dark, literally and figuratively. His concept of what it means to be an adult sexual male is being formed by an industry that doesn't respect women or men.

> **Many children are introduced to porn accidentally or unwillingly. And even those who seek out explicit content to answer some of their sexual questions have no idea what they are getting into. They have no moral or emotional template to process the sights and sounds they will experience.**

Porn's portrayal of manhood is leaving an imprint on the minds and souls of kids, tweens, and teens. Porn's story claims that sex is a weapon. Masculinity is all about power and control. Women are objects.

Porn Man lives in a world of narcissism, misogyny, and violence. He promotes a version of toxic manhood that eventually leads only to sexual, emotional, and spiritual poverty. Young males should enter adulthood with a "bank account" full of wisdom, maturity, tenderness, empathy, and emotional intelligence, but porn deposits only misogyny, aggression, and greed.

As pornography has trespassed into our lives through televisions, computers, tablets, and smartphones, it has colonized the sexuality of a generation of boys (and girls). In scene after scene, men pound women in hardcore, body-punishing sex. They invade every orifice of women's bodies while degrading them as "sluts," "whores," and "bitches." Then they ejaculate on the faces of their "victims."

For too many young males, this is the instruction manual on how to think about women, how to think about sex, and how to think about manhood.

These ideas are pressed into the wet concrete of boys' developing minds during key formative years. The parts of the brain that provide critical thinking are not fully developed. In other words, our children are largely defenseless against the onslaught of the porn story's sights and sounds. (Keep in mind that the brain's frontal lobes [its decision-making and reasoning center] aren't fully developed until one's mid-20s.)

What's more, most boys have little or no sexual history to draw upon. They have no context to help them interpret what they are seeing and reject the harmful depictions. Thus, porn's story represents normal sexual behavior to them, because it's the only sexual behavior they are aware of. Not surprisingly, 53 percent of teens self-report that pornography has impacted their sexual attitudes and behavior.[91]

Indeed, a lack of respect and empathy for women has become a hallmark of modern masculinity for the young porn consumer. A survey of 4,564 male teens (ages 14 to 17) revealed that those who regularly watched online porn were significantly more likely to hold negative gender attitudes.[92]

Now that we have explored how exposure to hardcore

pornography is affecting young males, let's take a closer look at how growing up in the digital porn age is affecting girls and young women.

Female Sexual Initiation

Porn is shaping many girls' perception of what it means to become a woman.

To place this impact in context, it's important to remember that, historically, women of all races and ethnicities have endured decades and decades of oppression. Women have needed to organize and mobilize just to secure basic human freedoms, such as the right to vote, own property, and earn equal wages. They have fought for the right to keep the wages they earned, leave an abusive marriage, or pursue traditionally "male" careers like medicine, law, or the military.

Much progress has been made, but some women still fight for basic freedoms like driving a car, dressing as they choose, and marrying whom they choose. Because women have been fighting oppression for so long, they yearn for empowerment.

Enter the porn industry. Porn claims its women are sexy and empowered. After all, female porn performers are typically better known and better paid than their male counterparts. In reality, however, porn represents everything women have been fighting against for centuries: subjugation, degradation, and inequality. Porn has sexualized oppression and subservience, while trying to disguise it as liberation.

Unfortunately, this false cover story is persuading too many young women. Let's explore why.

As a young girl reaches adolescence, she wants to be seen, heard, and valued. She wants to feel empowered. Like all humans, she yearns for validation. She wants to believe that she has something special to offer the world.

Meanwhile, she is also going through puberty, and all of the changes are lowering her self-esteem. She is vulnerable to the toxic messages of porn culture about what it means to be a modern, empowered female. Porn tells her, "You can enjoy the empowerment, validation, and social status you seek! Just use your body. Use your sexuality."

According to porn, sexualization is the road that leads to validation. But in porn's story, intelligent, business-savvy women are denigrated. They are considered threats. That's why a young girl who has been educated by porn might be more inspired by a pop star or internet influencer who exploits her sexuality than by an empowered female writer, political leader, or Supreme Court justice.

Pornography is impacting girls physically and psychologically. It is shaping their sexuality. Many young girls who are curious about sex (or who want to understand what their male peers are attracted to) search for answers in the Porn Universe. This is where they learn how to behave sexually—and what their boyfriends and society expect of them. They witness an array of violating and humiliating sexual scenarios they will be expected to comply with and "enjoy." They witness experiences billed as "sexually liberating and empowering." The reality, however, is quite the opposite.

When a young girl views porn, it can be arousing, frightening, and confusing. At first, she might be shocked or upset. Over time, however, graphic hardcore images become normalized. They start to become part of her sexual template. She is conditioned neurologically to get turned on by what she has witnessed. Eventually, her sexual appetites start to mirror those of the porn producers, rather than her own true desires for meaningful intimacy and connection.

In other words, she internalizes porn's misogynistic story. She inflicts it on herself. Perhaps that's why some women interviewed for this book reported that growing up on a porn diet of rough sex, bondage, rape simulations, and the like made them desire those things in their personal sex lives.

I don't believe these women were lying. They do desire such treatment, but that desire was conditioned. It doesn't truly reflect who they are as human beings.

Indeed, porn has literally rewired female sexual appetites and is creating what sociologists call a new "sexual template" for women. Porn is changing female sexual desires (via conditioning) and it begins early. Too early.

The ultimate result is women who fantasize about degradation, bondage, violent sex, rape, group sex, and more. Regardless of how a woman is being treated, porn's narrative requires that she must submit to all male domination. She will acquiesce to every act of aggression, regardless of how painful or humiliating it is. Females are being taught by porn that they should be submissive to male domination, that they should acquiesce to every male desire.

For example, in a 2015 study of 1,500 subjects, 52 percent of women reported that they had sexual fantasies of being tied up and forced into sex acts, 37 percent reported sexual fantasies of being whipped and slapped, and 29 percent reported fantasizing about being raped.[93]

Today's females aren't just pressured to act like Porn Woman; they must look like her too. They should have small frames but voluptuous breasts. They should carry no body fat and shave off all or most of their pubic hair. They might even need surgery to make their labia more attractive and symmetrical. (In 2017 there were more than 10,000 labiaplasty surgeries performed in the US.) The American Society of Plastic Surgeons reported that $17 billion was spent on cosmetic procedures in 2017. Ninety-two percent of these procedures were performed on females, with breast augmentation ranking number one.[94]

According to the report above, 87 percent of these surgeries are purely for cosmetic reasons, and some doctors are seeing a connection to porn. David Veale, a consultant psychiatrist in cognitive behavior therapy, links the surge in demand for labiaplasty surgery to increased porn exposure among women. "There is suspicion that this is related to much greater access to porn," he says, "so it is easier for women to compare themselves to actresses who may have had it done. This has to do with the increasing sexualization of society—it's the last part of the body to be changed."[95]

Dr. Norman Rowe, a Manhattan board-certified plastic surgeon, supports Veale's contention. Labiaplasty, he reports, is "the fastest-growing procedure out there. I don't see any stopping it."[96] The sad fact is that women are undergoing what the World Health Organization has defined as "female genital mutilation"[97] by the thousands, all because of the pressure to conform to porn's beauty ideal.

Dr. Jeffrey S. Palmer, the Director of the Cosmetic Urology Institute, reported, "I've seen an increase [in labiaplasty] in women of all ages, and especially in the much younger population, the 18-year-olds and sometimes younger than that."[98]

Dr. Debra Johnson, the Director of the American Society of Plastic Surgeons, reports that many young women request a labiaplasty because their boyfriend "doesn't like the way things look down there," because he is comparing what he sees to the porn he has grown up on.[99]

This is just one example of how porn's script is robbing a generation of females of an authentic and autonomous sexuality. It's part of porn's story of how young females should look and behave. Impressionable girls are conforming to the toxic story about their roles as women in the world—prefabricated females who do the bidding of prefabricated males, all to the detriment of everyone involved.

Unwanted Porn Exposure: A Form of Sexual Abuse

It's bad enough that pornographic content is inflicted on children, at ever-increasing rates. And studies show that much of this early exposure is inadvertent.[100]

Why is this important? Because unwanted sexual experiences are a form of sexual abuse. Many unsuspecting kids are assaulted with unsolicited pornographic images through search engines,[101] email messages, website sidebar ads, video-hosting websites (like YouTube),[102] social media sites (like Twitter, Instagram, TikTok, and Snapchat),[103] smartphone app ads, private social media messages,[104] instant messaging and private chat rooms,[105] interactive gaming, pop-ups, peer-to-peer file-sharing websites, virtual private networks (VPNs), and microblogging/social networking sites (like Tumblr), just to name a few.[106]

The Kaiser Family Foundation has reported that more than two-thirds of 15- to 17-year-olds have seen porn without intending to. Most of them said they were "very" or "somewhat" upset by what they viewed.[107] Indeed, such exposure to porn can prove to be a traumatic event in a kid's life.

Consider the case of Jonathan, who endured a long battle with a porn addiction. Jonathan sat in front of me and recalled his introduction to porn. He spoke quickly, and his voice cracked as he revealed, "I was first exposed to porn when I was twelve, and it was a very shocking experience.... I mean, it was a traumatic experience; when I was exposed to pornography it was traumatic for me.... I can't even describe it. It was like a wave hit me. I didn't know what to do. I felt two things immediately. One was a kind of fear/guilt combination.

It was scary. I didn't know what I was looking at. I didn't know how to interpret that. I felt like I needed to look over my shoulder, like I'm getting away with something, even though I didn't know what it was.

"I felt this immediate sense of something stirring in me; I didn't know what it was. It felt good, but it was like a rush. It was traumatic in the sense that my system was completely overwhelmed with stuff I couldn't handle: emotions, sexual feelings, thoughts, questions, confusion. I mean, it was just overwhelming my system."[108]

Jonathan's experience is not unique. For many young kids, the first exposure to porn is processed as trauma. That's because viewing porn is a sexual experience, just as real to a young brain as physical sexual contact. Research has revealed how our brains' "mirror neurons" respond powerfully to what we see and hear through entertainment. They react as if what we see on the screen (large or small) is actually happening to us.

These mirror cells were discovered in the mid-1990s, when a team of Italian scientists identified a phenomenon in the brains of macaque monkeys. The researchers observed that a monkey watching one of its peers grabbing a peanut experienced the same neural activity as when that monkey actually grabbed a peanut.

One of the researchers, neuroscientist Giacomo Rizzolatti, concluded that "if watching an action and performing that action can activate the same parts of the brain in monkeys—down to a single neuron—then it makes sense that watching an action and performing an action could also elicit the same feelings in people."[109]

Indeed it does, according to neuroscientist/neurosurgeon Donald Hilton, who maintains that "viewing other humans experience sexuality is sexuality to the viewer."[110]

In an interview for this book, William Struthers, researcher, psychologist, and author of *Wired for Intimacy*, explained, "The way mirror neurons systems work is that if I raise my hand, the part of your brain that would be involved in raising your hand is activated. Mirror neurons create a vicarious experience whereby watching something causes the same reactions in the brain that actually participating in the action would."[111]

Consider the implications for an 11-year-old boy or girl who stumbles on hardcore pornography and encounters content he or she won't ever be able to forget. In 1970, Thomas Emerson, a legal theorist who was a major architect of civil liberties laws, said that imposing what he called "erotic material" on individuals against their will is an act that "has all the characteristics of a physical assault."[112]

The definition of rape has been long debated. However, there is general agreement that sexual assault is non-consensual. Childhood exposure to pornography certainly fits this classification. As we have seen, many children are introduced to porn accidentally or unwillingly. And even those who seek out explicit content to answer some of their sexual questions have no idea what they are getting into. They have no moral or emotional template to process the sights and sounds they will experience.

Children's frequent and continued exposure to porn is a crisis. It's harming our kids in myriad ways. It's a perverse and unrealistic initiation into adulthood. It presents a deformed image of masculinity and femininity. It's a neurological sexual assault. It's an injustice against children. And it lures many young people into a porn addiction that might plague them for life. Too many kids grow into adults who find themselves trapped in the story of porn.

6

TRAPPED IN THE STORY OF PORN

*"I was mortified by the prospect of becoming
hopelessly trapped in someone else's story."*

—LIONEL SHRIVER, [113]
We Need to Talk About Kevin

magine you are standing across the street from an elementary
school playground. You hear a bell ring. Doors fling open and
dozens and dozens of children flood out for recess. They play
foursquare and tag. They shoot baskets and navigate the jungle gym.

Next, you notice a flashy sports car enter the parking lot. An
attractive man in a stylish suit exits the car. You regard him with
suspicion.

Carrying a colorful children's backpack, he walks purposefully
toward the playground. He glides past a distracted playground monitor. He finds a spot in the middle of the playground and starts to
distribute free candy. Then he produces a bag of white powder. It's
probably cocaine, you suspect. He tells the kids, "Try putting a little
of this on your candy." They eagerly hold out their pieces of candy
to him.

How would you feel about this scenario unfolding before your eyes? How long would it take you to call the police, alert someone at the school, or confront the man yourself?

Yet every day the same scenario takes place right under our noses. The substance in question is as harmful as any hard drug on the market. It has been proven to damage a child's sexual, mental, emotional, and physical health. And no candy man is needed to distribute it, because the drug is already present on the digital playground that most children frequent every day.

Dr. Jeffrey Satinover is a Harvard- and Yale-educated psychiatrist, psychoanalyst, and physicist who has testified before Congress about the insidious and addictive power of porn. He says that, because of the internet, "the delivery system for this addictive stimulus has become nearly resistance-free. It is usable in the privacy of one's own home and injected directly into the brain through the eyes. It's now available in unlimited supply via a self-replicating distribution network, glorified as art, and protected by the Constitution."[114]

It's no wonder that so many people find themselves trapped in the story of porn. And to truly appreciate the danger of this trap, we need to understand the nature of addiction. According to the American Psychiatric Association (APA), addiction is "a complex condition, a brain disease that is manifested by compulsive substance use despite harmful consequence."[115] The APA adds that, "like other chronic diseases, addiction often involves cycles of relapse and remission."

The American Society of Addiction Medicine defines addiction as a "chronic disease of brain reward, motivation, memory, and related circuitry." The ASAM adds that addicts often find themselves "pathologically pursuing" the substance or behavior that produces reward or relief.[116]

With the above definitions in mind, let's summarize what psychiatrists and other medical professionals have learned about addiction:

- Addiction is a brain disease or dysfunction.

- It involves a pathological pursuit of reward from a substance or behavior.

- It is characterized by an inability to abstain.

- It often involves cycles of relapse and remission.

To understand how the above factors can affect behavior, we need to look to some rats.

Understanding the "Reward Circuitry" of the Brain

Did you know that a rat's brain is very similar to that of a human? Researchers have known this (or at least suspected it) for a long time. In the late 1930s, psychologist and researcher B. F. Skinner used an experimental chamber (which came to be known as the "Skinner box") to observe the effects of punishment and reward. He used rats (and pigeons) as his subjects. He found that rats quickly learned to press a lever to avoid punishment (an electrical shock) or earn food.

In the 1950s, a group of researchers modified the box so that a "lever press" would deliver direct brain stimulation through deeply implanted brain electrodes. David Linden, professor of neuroscience at The Johns Hopkins University School of Medicine and author of *The Compass of Pleasure: How Our Brains Make Fatty Foods, Orgasm, Exercise, Marijuana, Generosity, Vodka, Learning, and Gambling Feel So Good*, summarized, "What resulted was perhaps the most dramatic experiment in the history of behavioral neuroscience: Rats would press the lever as many as 7,000 times per hour to stimulate their brains."[117]

The researchers discovered that the brain contains a pleasure center, a "reward circuit." This circuit involves several areas of the brain, including the nucleus accumbens (which receives dopamine); the hippocampus* (which stores episodic memories based on specific events); the VTA (the ventral tegmental area), which is home to dopaminergic cell bodies of the mesocorticolimbic dopamine system and other dopamine pathways; the prefrontal cortex (responsible for controlling behavior); and the amygdala (the "fight or flight" center).

Here's how Linden describes the power of the brain's reward circuitry and the intensity of rats' compulsion to push a "pleasure lever": "A series of subsequent experiments revealed that rats preferred pleasure circuit stimulation to food (even when they were hungry) and water (even when they were thirsty). Self-stimulating male rats would ignore a female in heat and would repeatedly cross foot-shock-delivering floor grids to reach the lever. Female rats would abandon their newborn nursing pups to continually press the lever. Some rats would self-stimulate thousands of times per hour for 24 hours, to the exclusion of all other activities. They had to be unhooked from the apparatus to prevent death by self-starvation. Pressing that lever became their entire world."[118]

Given the results of this experiment and others like it, it's no wonder that the discovery of the power of the brain's reward circuitry (also known as the mesolimbic pathway) has revolutionized our understanding of learning, pleasure seeking, and addiction. (This circuit is referred to as a "dopaminergic" pathway, because it is powered by the neurotransmitter called dopamine.)

---

* The hippocampus is the foundation of memory in the brain and part of the reward circuit. It preserves agreeable memories that are associated with a pleasurable stimulus, and, by association, it also preserves all of the details of the environment in which this pleasurable stimulus was received. Later, similar environments can recall the pleasurable memories preserved by the hippocampus and trigger a strong desire for the "reward" or pleasure.

Rats were willing to go to extremes to get their dopamine high—a high produced by stimulating their brains, not by any drug or chemical substance. This is significant because our behaviors can trigger a brain chemical release—and the subsequent responses.

How does this relate to addiction? As a behavior becomes more ingrained, we build up a tolerance to its effects. (Think of an addict who needs more and more of an opiate to achieve a high.)

Some call this process a hijacking of the brain's reward circuitry. When our brains are hijacked, a healthy behavior (like eating three healthy meals daily) can spiral into something unhealthy (like binge eating).

Let's take a closer look at this hijacking process:

First, let's note that the cerebrum (or forebrain) constitutes 85 percent of the brain's weight. The cerebrum is covered by a sheet of neural tissue known as the cerebral cortex, which envelops other brain structures and is divided into lobes. The cerebral cortex plays a key role in memory, attention, perceptual awareness, thought, language, and consciousness.

If you were to look at the cerebral cortex under a powerful microscope, you would see billions of tiny cells—called neurons—that communicate with one another. (The human brain contains about 100 billion neurons.)

As we experience life, our neurons learn to communicate and work together, forming our neural networks and pathways. This communication happens via synaptic transmission, also called neurotransmission or neuronal firing. Picture one brain cell releasing a chemical (neurotransmitter) and the next brain cell absorbing it, time after time after time.

Addiction and Brain Chemistry

Dopamine is one of the most important and potent neurotransmitters (or chemical messengers). In the normal communication process, dopamine is released by a neuron into the synapse (the small gap between neurons). Then it binds or connects with dopamine receptors on the neighboring neuron. It's a pitch and catch, one that creates habits.

Dr. Donald Hebb, a Canadian neuropsychologist known for his work in the field of associative learning, described the process with the phrase, "Neurons that fire together, wire together."[119] This "wiring together" of neurons results in habits and behavioral patterns. As we've seen, these patterns can become addictions when an action is paired with pleasure, and repeated time after time. The brain can create a pattern that is so easy to repeat that it becomes almost automatic.

Here's a simple example: When was the last time you gave deep thought to tying your shoes? We all fumbled and stumbled with this task when we first learned it, but it's now automatic. We can do it while carrying on a conversation or watching TV.

However, we don't become addicted to tying our shoes, because it's not a particularly pleasurable task. And it doesn't have detrimental consequences (unless you do it wrong).

But what happens when a behavior or substance is addictive? According to Harvard Medical School: [R]epeated exposure to an addictive substance or behavior causes nerve cells . . . to communicate in a way that couples liking something with wanting it, in turn driving us to go after it. That is, this process motivates us to take action to seek out the source of pleasure."[120]

In other words, when we engage in a behavior like porn use, which causes pleasure (like orgasm or excitement), our brain cells communicate—or "fire"—together frequently, and the connection between them strengthens. Messages that travel the same pathway in the brain over and over begin to transmit faster and faster, creating "networks." (Imagine tiny workers in your brain, constructing dirt trails, then a superhighway, then a high-speed light-rail system.)

Because of our brains' system of networks, we don't have to "learn" things over and over again (like how to tie our shoes, drive a car, or memorize our multiplication tables). This changing of the brain by linking neurons together into certain pathways and networks is called "neuroplasticity," a fancy word for the brain's ability to change or be molded, just like plastic.

Our neural networks control the flow of information, emotions, and sensations. They also allow us to form memories and learn new skills. In the process, our brains change physically. This is why certain behaviors (like porn consumption) become so ingrained that we feel a deep physical and psychological need for them.

This is how addictions are born: addictions to drugs, alcohol, gambling, and, yes, porn. A drug addict and a porn addict both experience chemical changes in the brain. The only difference is that one addict reacts to a chemical produced in a laboratory, while the other reacts to a chemical produced in his brain.

Dr. Donald Hilton, whom we met in the previous chapter, explains this phenomenon with a personal anecdote:

> I would like to share an experience our family had a few years ago on a safari in Africa. On the way to our camp on the Zambezi River, we stayed at Victoria Falls. The beauty of the falls was captivating as the Zambezi plunged 360 feet into the gorge below. At our camp on the river, we were cautioned that while beautiful, the river held dangers. Hippos and crocodiles were plentiful, and we were told to exercise caution around the water. While on a game drive along the river, our ranger commented

on the adrenaline grass growing along the banks. I asked him why he used the word adrenaline, and he began to drive slowly through the grass.

Abruptly he stopped the Land Rover and said, "There! Do you see it?"

"See what?" I asked.

He drove closer. Then I understood. A lion was hiding in the grass, watching the river, just waiting for some "fast food" to come get a drink. We were told that if we stayed in our seat and remained still, the lion would look at the Land Rover as a whole and not see us as individuals, and fortunately this was the case for us.

As far as the word adrenaline—we were sitting in open air Land Rovers with no doors and no windows. I then understood why it was called adrenaline grass as I felt my heart pound. My cerebral cortex saw and defined the danger, which registered in the autonomic, or automatic, part of the nervous system. The brain, which is a very efficient pharmaceutical lab, produced the chemical adrenaline. This brain drug caused my heart to pound and race in preparation for survival. I was ready to run if needed, not that it would have done any good with the lion.

Interestingly, adrenaline, also called epinephrine, is a drug we physicians use in surgery and in emergencies to start the heart again when it beats too slow, or even stops.

So, is epinephrine not a drug if the brain makes it and it causes the heart to pound and race, yet is a drug if the same epinephrine is given by a physician?

What about dopamine? This chemical is a close cousin to epinephrine, and for you chemists out there, it differs from epinephrine only by a methyl group. They are excitatory neurotransmitters which tell the brain to "Go!" Dopamine is important in the parts of our brain that allow us to move, and when the dopamine-producing parts of the brain are damaged, Parkinson's Disease results. To treat Parkinson's Disease, physicians prescribe dopamine as a drug, and it helps the person to move again.

So, is it a drug only if the pharmaceutical lab makes it, and not if the brain makes the same chemical for the same purpose?

Of course, both are drugs in every sense of the word, regardless of where they are produced.[121]

Indeed, our current understanding of the brain's reward circuitry and chemistry helps us understand why porn can become as addictive as narcotics, nicotine, or alcohol.

For example, one study found that the over-consumption of "natural rewards" (like sex and food) increases DeltaFosB, a protein that is abundant in the neurons of addicted people. DeltaFosB has been described as "the master switch" that triggers addiction-related changes in the brain. This "master control" protein was discovered in the neurons of animals during drug-addiction research.[122]

In another study (published in the journal *Biological Psychiatry*), researchers demonstrated that the over-consumption of natural rewards was shown to cause changes in neurons in the nucleus accumbens, like those changes seen with drugs of abuse.[123]

Debunking the Myth "There's No Such Thing as Porn Addiction"

The World Health Organization's International Classification of Diseases (11th edition) included a diagnosis for "Compulsive sexual behavior disorder,"[124] an umbrella term for sex addiction. Sex addiction is a potent phenomenon. A study published in the *Journal of Neuroscience* found that sexual climax rivals a heroin rush in the intensity of its pleasure reward in the brain.[125] (Think back to the example of the rats pushing levers to get their pleasure rewards.)

Sex and sexual climax produce a powerful release of pleasure chemicals in the brain, including a strong surge of dopamine. In the context of intimate, relational, person-to-person sexual interaction, this rush of pleasure chemicals is a normal and healthy phenomenon. However, when viewing porn frequently and masturbating often to intensely stimulating and novel visuals (or other activities that are considered hyper-sexual), one's brain reward circuitry can spiral out of control. This can result in sexual addictions that are characterized by compulsion and the need for edgier and edgier material or behaviors to get the same rush of sexual reward.

Our current understanding of the brain's reward circuitry and chemistry helps us understand why porn can become as addictive as narcotics, nicotine, or alcohol. Multiple studies have shown addiction-related brain changes in porn users and sex addicts.

In 2007, a German study revealed that sexual compulsion produces the same effects as cocaine, methamphetamine, and binge eating.[126] Another study concluded that a sexual compulsion can cause physical, anatomical changes in the brain, and these changes are a common thread in those suffering from addiction.[127]

That's why many researchers agree that "chronic consumption" of pornography is one form of sexual compulsion or hypersexuality. Using MRI scans, scientists at Cambridge University found changes in the brains of compulsive porn users. Specifically, these researchers found that compulsive and frequent pornography use produces the same brain activity as abusing alcohol or drugs.

Dr. Valerie Voon, a neuropsychiatrist and neuroscientist at the University of Cambridge, explained, "When an alcoholic sees an ad for a drink, their brain will light up in a certain way, and they will be stimulated in a certain way. We are seeing this same kind of activity in users of pornography."[128]

Psychologist and author Philip Zimbardo agrees: "When excessive porn viewing becomes addictive, the brain lights up as if it were on heroin."[129]

In addition to the study above, Berlin-based researchers Simone Kühn and Jürgen Gallinat explored porn-induced brain changes and addiction. The duo studied 64 men ages 21 to 45 and asked about their consumption of pornography. Then, with the help of MRIs, the researchers recorded brain structure and brain activities while the subjects viewed pornographic images. The scans revealed a connection between the number of hours the subjects spent viewing pornographic material per week and the overall volume of gray matter in their brains. The more the subjects were exposed to pornography, the smaller the volume of their gray matter.

"This could mean that regular consumption of pornography dulls the reward system, as it were," said Kühn, the leader of the study (and a scientist in developmental psychology research at the Max Planck Institute for Human Development).[130]

It is worth noting that at least 36 other studies have found addiction-related brain changes in porn users and sex addicts. In his book *The Brain That Changes Itself*, psychiatrist Norman Doidge explains: "The men at their computers looking at porn . . . had been seduced into pornographic training sessions that met all the conditions required for plastic change of brain maps. Since neurons that fire together wire together, these men got massive amounts of practice wiring these images into the pleasure centres* of the

---

* Dr. Doidge is Canadian, so we have used his spelling.

brain, with the rapt attention necessary for plastic change. . . . Each time they felt sexual excitement and had an orgasm when they masturbated, a 'spritz of dopamine,' the reward neurotransmitter, consolidated the connections made in the brain during the sessions. Not only did the reward facilitate the behaviour; it provoked none of the embarrassment they felt purchasing *Playboy* at a store. Here was a behaviour with no 'punishment,' only reward. The content of what they found exciting changed as the Web sites introduced themes and scripts that altered their brains without their awareness. Because plasticity is competitive, the brain maps for new, exciting images increased at the expense of what had previously attracted them—the reason, I believe, they began to find their girlfriends less of a turn-on."[131]

Given these facts, it's no wonder that some doctors are treating porn addicts with some of the same drugs used on drug addicts. In 2008, for example, Dr. Michael Bostwick and Dr. Jennifer Bucci produced a report out of the Mayo Clinic on their experimental treatment of internet pornography addiction with the drug naltrexone (a drug used to treat opiate addicts).[132]

Addictive Materials in the Hands of Our Kids

So, if porn is addictive—just as drugs, nicotine, alcohol, gambling, and overeating can be—what does that mean for the many adolescents who have been exposed to porn?

First, most addictive substances come with age limits or other barriers to access. Porn is an exception. For the most part, there are no meaningful legal restraints for children.[133] Yes, some porn sites provide age-limit warnings and "restrictions," but a child doesn't even need to be tech-savvy to press the onscreen button that says, "I certify that I am over 18."

And let's keep in mind that the brain's prefrontal cortex is not fully developed until a person is in his or her mid-20s. This region of the brain is responsible for judgment, decision-making, weighing cost/benefit, and so on. The prefrontal cortex allows humans to make strategic decisions, rather than compulsive ones.[134]

For example, your brain's pleasure center—driven by dopamine—might tell you to eat a gallon of ice cream because ice cream is delicious. But then your frontal lobe weighs in. It reminds you that, while ice cream is delectable, it's also high in saturated fat, sugar, and calories. Plus, bingeing on ice cream will sabotage the diet you have been faithfully following for two weeks.

The result? You leave the ice cream in the freezer because your frontal lobe has overruled your "pleasure center."

You have considered important long-term implications, goals, and commitments, not just a momentary thrill. Imaging studies comparing brain activity among children, teenagers, and adults showed that teenagers have exaggerated responses to medium and large rewards (pleasures), compared to young children and adults. Also, teens show little response to small rewards, unlike young children and adults.

Consider a young child who is delighted when you make a silly face at him, or when he notices a colorful butterfly nearby. These small rewards, however, would have little effect on a typical teenager. A teen needs much stronger pleasures or "rewards" to elicit a response, and the teen brain will seek those rewards with intensity. This combination of an underdeveloped prefrontal cortex and a strong desire for reward helps explain the stereotypical teen behavior that is often focused on pleasure above all else.

In other words, a teen's pleasure-seeking drive is full-throttle. But the reasoning part of his brain is stuck in first gear.

When teens access sexually stimulating pornographic content (available in endless variation), their pleasure centers rush them toward these intense rewards. There is little or no thought given to the consequences. Imagine a child alone in a candy store, with no one around to warn him of the consequences of devouring everything in sight.

All of the evidence points to the need for porn addiction to be recognized as a disease, just like alcohol or drug addiction.

Think of it this way: Cardiovascular disease damages the heart, and diabetes impairs the pancreas. Porn addiction hijacks the brain. It changes the brain's structure and function. Even worse, porn hijacks the relationships and interactions between men and women.

7

LIVING THE STORY OF PORN:
Hookup Culture

We live in an age where the youngest and most vulnerable among us are growing up on the story of porn. Porn initiates girls and boys into their lives as sexual beings. Many of them go on to become trapped in the narrative of porn's story, often for life.

Why? Because stories are powerful. They shape our most deeply held beliefs and values. They teach us how to feel and think about ourselves and others. And we know that the story of porn is a toxic soup of deformed masculinity, femininity, and sexuality.

We have explored porn's story about men, which says they exist to abuse, dominate, subjugate, and humiliate women for sexual pleasure—and to demonstrate their power. Men in porn are pathologically narcissistic and incapable of feeling emotion or empathy.

We have seen how porn portrays women as a subclass of humans who love to be sexually abused, dominated, subjugated, and humiliated. For Porn Woman, sex is a meaningless transaction, devoid of intimacy, care, or connection. And too often, porn sex is a vehicle for the physical, psychological, and emotional destruction of women at the hands of men.

The previous chapter revealed some of porn's physical effects, especially on our brains. But what about social effects? What happens to people who internalize porn's story? How does the near-universal ingestion of this story influence the way we think, and, more importantly, the way we behave?

First, let's consider some of the ways this toxic story seeps into our mass consciousness, shaping our attitudes about what it means to be a man, a woman, and a sexual being—creating what we'll call a "porn culture." In this culture, the constant barrage of pornographic images becomes, as we learned earlier, "the wallpaper of our lives."

What does it mean to grow up in a porn culture? It means that we collectively fulfill the roles porn has scripted for us. Men and women are buying into porn's story about who they are and what sex is for—a story that is being perpetuated by the mass media. We live in a media-dominated society, and that's why porn's story is so hard to escape.

Consider Instagram star Dan Bilzerian, who boasts almost 33 million followers on the app. He has built his brand by surrounding himself with scores of scantily clad women. On an episode of the popular podcast *The Joe Rogan Experience*, Bilzerian bragged about sleeping with 16 women in 12 days, without even speaking to one of them. He also noted, "Sex for money is one of the most, like, pure interactions."

Rogan repeatedly praised Bilzerian, saying, "You're the number-one baller. I'm giving you the crown!"[135]

None of this is out of the ordinary. It is the norm for women to be presented as ornamental sex objects, and for men to be portrayed as serial predators whose primary purpose is to "hook up" with as many women as possible.

Porn's story, embraced and promoted by the Dan Bilzerians of the world, has made a significant impact on college campuses. These campuses are an eye-opening microcosm of the culture at large when it comes to ideas about masculinity, femininity, and sex. Here, we can see the "great social experiment" of mass porn culture played out in real time.

Porn Culture = Hookup Culture

The meaning of sex has completely changed for a generation of young people who have grown up on porn and porn culture. Non-relational, transactional sex is the norm for those who have come of age in a hypersexualized media culture. Talking about what sex means to them, two college males explained to me:

> Adam: It's just a commodity, really, isn't it?
> Shay: Today, sex is all about f**king getting it in.
> Adam: Yeah, sex is a number. What's your number?
> Shay: Don't know.
> Adam: (laughing) Neither do I.[136]

Gone are the days when college sexual experiences were part of finding love and a meaningful relationship. Professor Donna Freitas, author of *The End of Sex: How Hookup Culture is Leaving a Generation Unhappy, Sexually Unfulfilled, and Confused About Intimacy*, told me: "[A] lot of young women that I spoke to would say things like, 'I thought I would come to college and fall in love. . . . I thought that would happen to me, and now that I'm here, I realize that's not what people do anymore. Love isn't part of the college experience.'"[137]

When it comes to sex among college students, intimate connection, commitment, and emotion have been replaced by the "hookup," sex lacking any true feelings about your partner. There is no deep emotional connection. Many hookup partners don't even know one another's names. Or those names are quickly forgotten. Often, hookup partners never see each other or communicate again.

One college male told me, "Back in the past, it would usually be, you know, 'Let me take you on a date, let me get to know you a little bit before we take it any further.' Versus now—now it's like you get a girl's number and the majority of the guys here are just [interested in] sex."[138]

I asked another college guy if he would "get to know" a girl before having sex with her. His blunt answer: "What do you mean, get to know her? Yeah, I'll get to know her name, where she's from, that's about it. Then it's down to business."[139]

Casual sex is nothing new, of course. What is new? Sex with zero affection, caring, or empathy for another human being. This phenomenon has been termed "hookup culture" by sociologists. In this culture, a guy might have sex with Partner A, Partner B, and Partner C, perhaps all in the same night. No strings attached. One anonymous college female described it this way: "We meet on the beach, we get drunk, we go back to the hotel, we have casual sex, and then we go about our lives like we never met.... It's unrespectful [sic], whatever, but that's the way it works."

Another male college spring-breaker told me (anonymously): "People come to Panama City to basically get f**ked up and f**k bitches. That's it. We're trying to get laid."

Given that porn promotes a brand of sexuality devoid of commitment and intimacy, it is not surprising that college students who view porn frequently have an increased number of sexual partners and higher incidence of "hooking up."[140]

But hookup culture isn't limited to college campuses and spring-break beaches. Casual hookup sex now dominates society at large, especially among millennials and Generation Z'ers. We are living in the swipe right, swipe left generation. There are hookup apps for any type of sex you can imagine. We have apps like Grindr, Tinder, and CasualX and websites like Ashley Madison to facilitate no-strings-attached hookups. Porn is redefining how people experience sexuality, celebrating a brand of sex that is non-intimate, transactional, and meaningless.

One porn consumer confided, "I viewed pornography as a training manual for how I should be as a man, and how I should be in the bedroom, and how I should be relating to women."[141] Such is the power of porn's story to influence an entire generation's view of the value and meaning of sex. Porn is also influencing the type of sex people are having.

> "The porn industry is reshaping the social, emotional, and cognitive map of young people in ways that undermine healthy development, women's equality, and a sustainable culture."
>
> DR. GAIL DINES

A study published in the *Archives of Sexual Behavior* found that pornography creates a script that guides sexual experiences. The study found that the more pornography a man watches, the more likely he is to view it during sex, request particular pornographic sex acts of his partner, and deliberately conjure images of pornography during sex to maintain arousal.[142]

One porn producer told me, "With more and more people having their first encounter of sexual intercourse in pornography, this is shaping what we think sex is. . . . Boys start getting, from a very early age, a picture that this [pornography] is what sexuality is supposed to be like."[143]

Abusive, degrading sexual scenes are viewed over and over and over as a boy matures into a young man, each time firing the reward circuitry system of his brain. He starts to believe that "getting off" as fast as possible is the purpose of sex, and that sex is completely devoid of humanity or intimacy. Pornographers understand that the content they produce is shaping the way that an entire generation of consumers are engaging in sex.

One porn producer told me, "I think porn has an impact on guys as far as how they perform sexually with women. I don't think years ago, you would see a guy taking a girl out to a date and on the third date he tries to do a piledriver [extreme sexual position] with her. You know, these things didn't happen.... I never saw that happening.... I think [porn has] shaped the way that guys and girls participate in sex. It's turned it more into, you know, life imitating art."[144]

Indeed, those who run the porn industry have co-opted our sexuality, promoting things like gangbangs, orgies, and "hookup" sex between strangers. As sociologist Gail Dines noted in her interview for this book, the porn industry is "reshaping the social, emotional, and cognitive map of young people in ways that undermine healthy development, women's equality, and a sustainable culture."[145]

Additionally, 75 percent of sex buyers (e.g., customers of prostitution) say they received their sex education from pornography, according to a study conducted by Melissa Farley, clinical psychologist and director of Prostitution Research & Education, a San Francisco-based nonprofit organization. The study also found that sex buyers use significantly more pornography than nonbuyers.[146]

Hookup culture is thriving because porn has taught us to see sex as a meaningless transaction. Somehow, we have bought into the story that porn has scripted for us. And we act it out to our great detriment.

8

LIVING THE STORY OF PORN:
Rape Culture

The sheer amount of sexual violation of women and girls today is staggering. One in five—or 64 million Americans—have reported experiencing rape or attempted rape.[147] One in four female undergraduate students are sexually assaulted while attending college.[148] On a global level, nearly one-third (30 percent) of women have experienced physical and/or sexual violence.[149]

According to UNICEF, approximately 120 million girls worldwide—slightly more than one in ten—have experienced forced intercourse or other forced sexual acts at some point in their lives.[150]

While filming a documentary on hookup culture (and working on the previous chapter), I spent time at popular spring-break destinations, talking to young people about their sexual ethos. Young adults spoke with me about their casual view of sex, the dominance of hookup culture, and the ways young men and women gain validation (by accumulating sexual partners, winning "hot body" contests, etc.). None of this surprised me.

However, I was not prepared to view the rampant sexual assault that I witnessed day after day. In fact, during five years' worth of spring breaks, I didn't meet even one young woman who had not been sexually violated in some way. Young woman after young woman confided to me, "Some guy walked up and started sucking my tit," or "Some guy pulled down my bikini bottoms in the crowd and tried to finger me." And these were not the worst things I heard.

What I observed at parties mirrored what the various spring-breakers were telling me:

A young woman was placed on a guy's shoulders and was instantly swarmed by young men chanting things like, "Show your tits!" and "Suck our dicks!"

I saw guys rip women's clothes off, grab their breasts, and demand various sex acts. I witnessed mob after mob of hyper-aggressive young men who believed they were entitled to a woman's body. When I asked them how the girls felt about being treated this way, they responded, "They want it!"

> "We know it to be a fact that pornography contributes to the battering of women and children."
>
> DONNA DUNN, Minnesota Coalition for Battered Women

This behavior reflects a key theme of the porn story: Women exist to satisfy men's sexual desires, so a man has the right to use a woman sexually. It's the path to pleasure and dominance, and the admiration of one's male peers.

Men gain approval by pursuing and "conquering" as many women as possible. This mindset creates predatory sexual strategies designed to veto a woman's "no." Her desires and her dignity are not even considered.

Males who grow up on the story of porn don't know how to engage in a sexual relationship based on agency and mutual respect and consideration. A female who has passed out from too much alcohol represents an invitation to a sexual conquest, rather than a cry for help.

The entitled male attitude toward women's bodies was on full display during the polarizing rape case in Steubenville, Ohio. A group of teens, led by Ma'lik Richmond and Trent Mays, dragged a vulnerable 16-year-old high school girl (who was intoxicated and unconscious) from party to party, sexually assaulting her and urinating on her repeatedly.

The most disturbing feature of this case was that these adolescents didn't believe that they were doing wrong. They filmed and photographed the entire ordeal and circulated the images through Facebook and Twitter. They reveled in something that should have brought them shame. Richmond and Mays were tried as juveniles and convicted of rape and, because of their victim's age, dissemination of child pornography.[151]

I learned more about rape culture and its connection to pornography one evening as I drove Sunset Boulevard with porn actor Eric Swiss (whom we met earlier in the book). He told me about picking up a girl at a nearby club. In fact, he confessed to meeting two intoxicated young women, whom he planned to take home. However, a random male joined them and offered to let them hang out in his hotel room.

Swiss reported that the group arrived at the hotel room, where he started making out with one of the girls. Suddenly, he heard a loud thumping noise coming from the adjacent bed. He looked over and saw that the other girl was unconscious. The noise was her head slamming into the headboard as the stranger was raping her.

Swiss told his "partner," "Hey, I think your friend is being raped." She replied, "Yeah, it happens." Then she resumed kissing him. After sharing this story, Swiss turned to me and said:

This is a big, nasty city you're in. . . . I don't know
where you're from, but there's twenty million people
fighting for their own piece of the pie right here. Dudes
get shot; bitches get raped. There are girls who go out,
drink themselves stupid, get raped, wake up the next
morning, brush their teeth, and go on about their lives.
There are guys who go to clubs, find wasted girls, take
advantage of them, brush their teeth, and go on with
their lives.[152]

To Swiss's point, many men regard consent as optional in their
sexual encounters. In their minds, no doesn't really mean no. In
one study of university students, 69 percent of US females reported
being subjected to at least one form of sexual coercion. Another study,
reported in the *Los Angeles Times,* noted that one in 16 US women
were forced or coerced into losing their virginity.[153]

Perhaps there is no better representative of the entitlement
mindset than Harvey Weinstein, once the most powerful man in
Hollywood. Weinstein's public downfall culminated with his arrest,
after *The New Yorker* (in its October 23, 2017 issue) broke the story
of his decades of sexual assault and manipulation.[154] His offenses
ranged from criminal sexual assault in the first degree to aggravated
rape. In other instances, he pressured actresses into sex scenes they
didn't want to do, so he could watch.

The stories that emerged revealed how Weinstein thought about
women, as well as the tactics he used to coerce and force them into
unwanted sexual encounters. He wielded his power to sexually
subjugate and dominate his victims. Harvey Weinstein is a classic
example of the male entitlement mindset, which is portrayed again
and again in modern porn.

Men like Weinstein (or R. Kelly or Bill Cosby) don't wake up one
day and commit sexual assault and rape. They go through a process

of socialization, starting as young children, which builds their belief system about who they are and what women are for. Ultimately, those beliefs influence and enable their behavior.

Given what we have learned in this chapter, it should surprise no one that adult film performer Ron Jeremy has been indicted on 34 counts of sex crimes, involving 21 women and spanning more than 20 years. According to prosecutors, Jeremy's victims ranged in age from 15 to 51. Jeremy, who appeared in more than 1,700 porn films, faces more than 300 years in prison. According to his indictment, the charges against him include 12 counts of rape, including that of a 17-year-old girl and a 15-year-old girl. He has pleaded not guilty to all charges.[155]

Permission-Giving Beliefs

I thought about the attitudes and behaviors of people like Weinstein and Jeremy when I interviewed a young man named Shay. Here's what he told me:

> The message I got from pornography is there is one very simple, biased way of treating women. They are [of] lesser value, and they are the property of men. They are there for his pleasure. These were my first concepts and ideas about what it meant to be a sexual being. . . . I guess it played out in my life at different stages.
>
> It was a real thread through my [early] life and even during my time in college—the way my guy friends, when we were together, would talk about women. We would have this banter with one another. It would be extremely degrading. We wouldn't see them as friends or equals but more something to conquer, to sleep with. . . .
>
> It was normal for us to try and push past their "no" and break down their resistance. Get further and further

and progress more and more with them. As soon as you have, maybe flirted with someone, got them back to your room, you are instantly pushing their boundaries to sleep with them. If you can sleep with them, now you got another number, another notch in the belt. Moving up in this ranking in the black book. At the time, I thought that was cool. I was consumed with the idea that you use women as objects to boost your own status. I look back at it; it was really sickening, but at the time, it was fun, and we were laughing about it. It was like a game for us. . . . We didn't see these women as human beings, so to speak; we saw them merely as a number.[156]

Men behave this way due to what sociologists call "permission-giving beliefs." They believe they have permission to act out, and porn consumption creates such beliefs in the minds of consumers. A 2011 study published in *Sexual Addiction & Compulsivity* analyzed the effects of pornography use on sexual attitudes and behaviors of college males. The researchers concluded:

College men's exposure to pornography is nearly universal, with growing viewing rates nationwide. Substantial research documents the harmful effects of mainstream, sadomasochistic, and rape pornography on men's attitudes and behavior related to sexual assault. The present study surveyed 62 percent of the fraternity population at a Midwestern public university on their pornography viewing habits, bystander efficacy, and bystander willingness to help in potential rape situations. Results showed that men who view pornography are significantly less likely to intervene as a bystander, report an increased behavioral intent to rape, and are more likely to believe rape myths [myths that women like and deserve rape].[157]

In the 1970s, the term "rape myths" was coined by Martha Burt to describe the attitude and beliefs of people about the act of rape, its perpetrators, and its victims. Burt wrote of "the importance of stereotypes and myths—deemed as prejudicial, stereotyped, or false beliefs about rape, rape victims, and rapists—in creating a climate hostile to rape victims."[158]

Rape myths are reflected in statements like these:

> "Only bad girls get raped."
> "Any healthy girl can resist a rapist if she really wants to."
> "She probably led him on."
> "She's just trying to get attention."[159]

In the case of Harvey Weinstein, such beliefs were reflected in comments like, "Why would he think he could get away with such behavior? Because there were women who took him up on his offer . . ." and "Men like Weinstein do what they do because there are men and women who are desperate enough to allow them to."[160]

Such myths reinforce the belief that women cause rape or deserve it—and that rapists are not responsible for their actions because they are overwhelmed by emotion, arousal, intoxication, etc. These myths point a finger at the women who were violated, while giving the men a pass.

Burt was one of the first researchers to investigate the impact of rape myths. She theorized that if men serving on a jury accepted the myths, they would be less sympathetic to rape victims and less likely to convict rapists. She also theorized that women who believe rape myths would be less likely to report rape as a crime or offer support to victims.

Research has proven the truth of Burt's theories, and it has shown links between porn consumption and rape myths.[161] In a study published in 1994 (before the explosion of internet porn), researcher Elizabeth Perse found that undergraduates who reported exposure to pornographic magazines and videos were more likely to believe that women deserved rape.[162]

Researchers Dolf Zillmann and Jennings Bryant reported that viewing even nonviolent pornography was positively correlated with the trivialization of rape and a lack of compassion for female victims.[163]

In 1995, a group of researchers conducted a meta-analysis of 24 rape myth acceptance studies (studies whose subjects totaled 4,268 people).[164] The researchers' analyses showed correlations between exposure to porn and an increased acceptance of the belief that women cause and deserve rape.[165] Other meta-analyses—by Kim and Hunter (1993a, 1993b);[166] Sheppard, Hartwick, and Warshaw (1988);[167] and Manning (2006)[168]—demonstrated the same connection between pornography consumption and the acceptance of rape myths. A variety of experimental research has replicated these findings.[169]

To put it simply: Sexually violent imagery changes men's and women's attitudes and behaviors about sexual assault. In a peer-reviewed study, males who viewed sexual violence scored higher on scales measuring the belief that women want and deserve rape, when compared to males who viewed violent films that were not sexual in nature.[170]

Even the father of "gonzo porn," John "Buttman" Stagliano, has pondered porn's role in perpetuating unhealthy attitudes and behaviors regarding sexual abuse. In 2006, he said the following at the Adult Video News (AVN) Expo:

[T]here's a lot more harder-edged stuff [today]; there's a lot more stuff that I would consider unpleasant to look at, that I personally don't like . . . that maybe feeds into a psychology that I don't think is healthy. . . . The psychology is that some people like to abuse other people, in real life, in real situations. And I worry that we're creating art that feeds on that, that kind of reinforces that and says it's a good thing, and makes people a little more comfortable with certain psychological things that I think they should be uncomfortable with.[171]

Researchers Milburn, Mather, and Conrad found that males who were shown scenes that sexually objectified and degraded women (and were then exposed to media that depicted rape) believed that the rape victim experienced pleasure and "got what she wanted."[172] Further, when serving on an experimental jury, study subjects who were exposed to pornography recommended a rape sentence that was half the sentence recommended by those who had not viewed pornographic imagery.[173]

Men who have bought into the rape myth and who have adopted permission-giving beliefs about sex and women are dangerous. But these beliefs are not limited to men. Many women who have grown up on porn have difficulty discerning the difference between a sexual encounter and a sexual assault. Research has found that women's early exposure to pornography brings consequences, including "rape fantasies" and beliefs that support the acceptability of rape.[174]

Of course, not all boys and men who watch porn will act out against women. But many do, and that's why we must continue to evaluate porn's role in perpetuating sexual violence. Think about the case of a 12-year-old boy who viewed pornography at a friend's house, via an Xbox 360 game console. After watching the pornography, he said he developed "a desire to try it out."

Over a period of a few months, he sexually assaulted his eight-year-old sister several times, eventually raping her.[175]

In New South Wales, Australia, porn-inspired child-on-child sexual offenses gained media attention when two 12-year-old boys raped a six-year-old girl in the bathroom of a primary school in Sydney. Peter Yeomans, the detective chief inspector of the NSW Child Abuse & Sex Crime Squad, warned that children were being "groomed" to be copycat perpetrators of sexual abuse by internet porn.[176]

Clearly, porn affects our beliefs about rape and sexual violence, and it also influences our behavior. A 2015 meta-analysis of 22 studies from seven countries found that the consumption of pornography was significantly associated with increases in verbal and physical aggression among males and females.[177]

The researchers in this project added that "the accumulated data leave little doubt that, on the average, individuals who consume pornography more frequently are more likely to hold attitudes conducive to sexual aggression and engage in actual acts of sexual aggression than individuals who do not consume pornography or who consume pornography less frequently."[178]

In another meta-analysis (comprising 12,323 subjects), researchers found that exposure to pornography significantly increases the risk for developing sexually deviant tendencies (by 31 percent) and committing sexual offenses (by 22 percent).[179]

The researchers concluded, "In order to promote a healthy and stable society, it is time that we attend to the culmination of sound empirical research [regarding these tendencies]."[180]

In one of the most thorough reviews of the experimental data, researcher Neil Malamuth and his colleagues concluded that "if a person has relatively aggressive sexual inclinations resulting from various personal and/or cultural factors. . .pornography exposure may activate and reinforce associated coercive tendencies and behaviors."[181]

Another study found that "all types of pornography (softcore, hardcore, violent, and rape) are correlated with using verbal coercion, drugs, and alcohol to sexually coerce women."[182]

And a study of deviant sexual behavior in children and young adolescents found that "twenty-nine of the thirty juveniles had been exposed to X-rated magazines or videos, and the average age of first exposure was about 7.5 years. . . . Those reporting higher exposure to violent pornography are six times more likely to report having raped than those reporting low exposure."[183]

As one might reason, adult sex offenders also report very high rates of hard-core pornography use. One study, conducted in (pre-internet) 1988, revealed: "Child molesters (sixty-seven percent), incest offenders (fifty-three percent), and rapists (eighty-three percent) were significantly higher in use than non-offenders (twenty-nine percent).[184]

Further, viewing degrading pornography increases dominating and harassing behavior toward women,[185] evokes harsher evaluations of real-life partners, and decreases compassion for female rape victims.[186]

Donna Dunn, who serves on the board of directors for the Minnesota Coalition for Battered Women, has asserted that "we at Women's Shelter, Inc. know it to be a fact that pornography contributes to the battering of women and children."[187]

The concept of "viewing and doing" takes an even darker turn when we consider how child sexual abuse material (CSAM) affects a person's beliefs and actions. In December 2017, USA Gymnastics doctor Larry Nassar was sentenced to 60 years in prison for the possession of thousands of images of child pornography.[188] In January of

2018 he was sentenced to 40 to 175 more years for the sexual abuse of more than 100 children and teens.[189]

Is this a coincidence? Research suggests otherwise.

Let's consider the 2009 "Butner Study,"[190] which was cited by the FBI (in testimony before Congress),[191] quoted in the US Attorney Bulletin,[192] and published in the peer-reviewed *Journal of Family Violence*. The study analyzed and compared the behaviors of 155 men (convicted of child pornography offenses) who participated in an intensive sex-offender-specific treatment program at a medium-security federal prison called FCC Butner.

By the end of the treatment period, 131 subjects (85 percent) admitted to at least one hands-on* sexual offense. The total number of reported victims among all offenders was 1,777, with an average of 13 victims per offender.[193] The study found that the men who possessed or distributed child-sexual-abuse images were extremely likely to have engaged in hands-on sexual abuse of a child.

Another study (conducted in 2003 and 2004) focused on 269 sexual offenders in the Colorado Department of Corrections system. Sixty-five percent of the child sexual abusers in the study group reported early exposure to pornography—before age 10. Among this group, the average age for the onset of child abuse was 14, and the average age for the onset of rape was 16. As for the victims, the average age of the children who were abused was 9; most were girls.[194]

Despite all of this compelling evidence, there are still those who deny porn's influence on beliefs and actions. For example, clinical psychologist and author David Ley promotes porn use, refuting the idea that porn adversely impacts one's behavior.

He contends that "we neglect our adolescents, and then punish them for learning about sexuality from the fantasy world of porn. If

---

* "Hands-on" was defined as "any fondling of children's genitals or breasts over clothing, as well as skin-to-skin contact including hand-to-genital, genital-to-genital, and genital-to-anus."

a child died from jumping off a building after watching *Superman*, we wouldn't blame the movie producer."[195] However, Ley's comments undermine his argument. Kids do watch *Superman* and act like Superman, because media is a powerful influencer. After watching *Peter Pan* enough times, a kid I know thought he was Peter. In fact, he carried around his plastic sword and wore his feathered hat for nearly a year. Visual media and internalized stories do impact beliefs and behavior. That's why the porn story's toxic messages are so harmful. If a child were to copy Superman, he might be inspired to save humanity. If he were to copy what he sees in porn, he might rape his little sister.

Media is unquestionably powerful. Advertisers know this. If visual media didn't affect our thoughts and behavior, would companies continue to pay millions of dollars for advertising slots during the Super Bowl or the Academy Awards? Of course not. McDonald's consistently spends over $900 million each year on visual advertising. Why? Because they know that media can change beliefs and behavior. This relationship has been described as the "media effect."[196] The visual media we consume impacts our lives, and porn is a powerful form of visual media.

The influence and power of porn's story extend to every realm of our personal and public lives, and this story impacts our most treasured relationships in ways that demand our observation and reflection.

Men and women worldwide are coming face to face with the porn story's effects on their intimate sexual relationships. That is where we must turn our attention next.

9

PORN'S STORY AND SEXUAL INTIMACY

*"I really didn't approach my wife as a person with whom
I could experience connection, but more as an object
who is there to gratify me—and it was all because of porn."*

—MICHAEL CUSICK, porn consumer[197]

om was 11 when he was first exposed to pornography. That set him on a trajectory of porn addiction for the next 20 years, and counting.

From a young age, Sarah decided to save sex for her wedding night. She often dreamed of her honeymoon, especially after she met Tom.

However, what Sarah encountered on her honeymoon (and during the first months of her marriage) was not the loving, mutually enjoyable sex she had always imagined.

In an interview for this book, she revealed, "The things that he wanted—sex acts—they were things that would make me feel humiliated. It was stuff about him being the powerful, dominant one and me being submissive. The things that he would ask me to do were things that made me feel like it was just about him getting off. There was no tenderness, but almost like an aggressiveness. It wasn't about love.

"I was just there for him to feel good. Things that he would ask of me would be very degrading, as if . . . there was not a concern for how it was making me feel. Further down the line, after I had found out about the pornography, I asked if the things he was asking me to do were things he had watched in porn—and they were."

Later in the interview, Sarah lamented about the degradation she felt as Tom demanded aggressive, dominating, and painful "porn sex."

"I felt like I was worthless to him," she said. She added that Tom had been so sexually conditioned by pornography that he was physically incapable of engaging in sex that was comfortable or enjoyable for her. He could not become aroused unless he dominated or humiliated her. Often, he had to injure her to achieve orgasm.

Sarah's attempts to discuss her concerns fell on deaf ears. Tom was so conditioned by the narrative of porn that he couldn't understand why his aggression bothered his wife. As she explained, "When I would confront him about the way it hurt me, he would say that he 'didn't get why' I would feel that way."

To Tom, who grew up on porn, his behavior was normal. As this book went to press, the future of Tom and Sarah's relationship was unclear. Some couples have been able to free themselves from the chains of the porn story, but others have not.

Why does sex play such a critical role in our intimate relationships? And why does it hurt so much when we experience sexual betrayal? Simply put, sex has value to us as human beings. It means something to us. That's why sexual infidelity is so devastating for people, regardless of their religious or cultural background.

Sex is the only way we experience complete physical, emotional, and spiritual connection. It is the only way we can wholly give ourselves to each other. Sexual intimacy connects us like nothing else.

Our bodies and brains are hardwired for intimacy and commitment. Advances in neuroscience have shown us the powerful brain chemicals that are released during sex. These chemical reactions connect us intimately, on a physical and emotional level. Oxytocin, the hormone that powerfully bonds a mother to her newborn child, is released during pregnancy, birth, and breastfeeding. It is also released during foreplay and orgasm.[198] It plays a key role in the emotional bonding of sexual partners,[199] and it builds feelings of trust.[200]

Vasopressin is another important hormone released in males after orgasm. As I mentioned in this book's preface, vasopressin is sometimes called "the monogamy molecule." Its role in monogamous, long-term relationships was discovered when scientists began to study the behaviors of the male prairie vole, a small biparental rodent common to the Midwest. Male prairie voles keep one sexual partner for life. They attack any vole who attempts to lure their mate away. However, when male prairie voles were given a drug that suppresses the effect of vasopressin, the bond with their partner deteriorated immediately. They lost their devotion to their mates and failed to protect them from new suitors.[201]

Further research on prairie voles indicated that vasopressin plays an important role in whether or not males participate in rearing offspring.[202] In her article "The Two Become One: The Role of Oxytocin and Vasopressin," Dianne S. Vadney (a teacher and family-ministry coordinator) wrote: "Essentially, vasopressin released after intercourse is significant in that it creates a desire in the male to stay with his mate, inspires a protective sense (in humans, perhaps this is what creates a jealous tendency) about his mate, and drives him to protect his territory and his offspring. The value of such tendencies toward the maintenance of marriage and family can easily be anticipated."[203] Like the prairie vole, humans are hardwired for intimate and long-term sexual connection.

In the words of neuroscientist Donald Hilton, "We are wired to bond to the object of our sexuality."[204] Perhaps that is why we are drawn to the stories of committed love between two sexual partners. Think about the classic movie *Love Story*. An unlikely couple falls in love and beats the odds after Oliver sacrifices his inheritance to marry Jenny. Their tender romance comes to a tragic end when Jenny discovers she is terminally ill. Oliver stays by her side until the end. He holds her tight, tears streaming down his face as she takes her last breath.

Or what about one of the most popular love stories of recent time, *The Notebook*? Who didn't choke up when Allie and Noah lay in each other's arms on their deathbed and said goodbye to the world together after a long life of intimate, passionate love?

Why do we love these stories? Perhaps because they resonate with our deep longing for intimate love, affection, and commitment. Most of us yearn to connect intimately with someone, "till death do us part." Unfortunately, porn's story is creating a sexuality that is non-intimate and temporary. Researcher J. P. Schneider's study of the spouses of cybersex addicts found that 68 percent of them experienced decreased sexual intimacy with their partner as a result of porn addictions.[205]

What's more, the spouses revealed that the decrease in intimacy began at the same time the porn viewing started. Schneider's study also found that half of the porn users eventually lost all interest in sex with their partners. In many cases, the porn consumer will develop cynicism about love or the need for affection, even developing a distaste for affection between romantic partners.[206]

One begins to believe that sexual pleasure doesn't require any affection or intimacy. After all, those feelings aren't present in the world of porn.[207]

Here are more results from Schneider's research:

1. Porn users blame their partners for sexual problems.

2. Porn users coerce their partners to engage in sexual acts they object to.

3. Porn users are less likely to initiate sex.

4. Porn users are emotionally detached during sex, and solely interested in their own pleasure.[208]

These results should be unsurprising by now. As we have seen, porn conditions males to view women as lesser humans or as objects that can be dominated and controlled for one's sexual pleasure.

We have already heard from women who felt objectified by their partners. As one woman lamented to researchers, "I am no longer a sexual person or partner to him, but a sexual object. He is not really with me, not really making love to me. . . . He seems to be thinking about something or someone else—likely those porn women. . . . He is just using me as a warm body."[209]

Such attitudes lead to a breakdown of the relationship. Many wives report a sense of shame and despair for not being able to "live up to" their husbands' expectations.[210]

A woman named Annie spoke to me about the impact of her partner's porn use: "The pressure that I felt to perform with him as a partner wasn't normal. I felt like I had to learn how to be a better sex partner. Like I had to do what they were doing on the screen. I had to hurt myself and do the sexual acts that I saw, different positions, whatever they were doing in the film. And extreme positions. Extreme oral positions that I had to do on him to make him happy."

Annie continued, "And the entire time I'm trying to please him, because I'm in love with him, I'm not getting any pleasure myself because I'm so worried about taking care of him and being all that

I can be, so that possibly he would say 'Oh, I don't need to watch this porn anymore. I can just shut it off. She's all I want. She's all I've ever dreamed about. This girl's perfect for me.' But that never happened."[211]

Because of dynamics like these, spouses of porn consumers feel rejected, unattractive, and sexually inadequate. Some become severely depressed.[212] Others suffer so much distress that they require clinical treatment for trauma.[213] In fact, surveys have shown that the more time women think their partners are spending viewing porn, the greater their feelings of anguish and despondency.[214]

In 2002, researchers Bergner and Bridges analyzed 100 letters posted to various online message boards for female partners of men who were frequent users of porn. The women consistently expressed despair over their partners' decreased sexual desire for them.

One woman wrote, "I am no longer sexually attractive or desirable to him. He's more attracted to the women depicted in his movies, magazines, and websites than he is to me, and I feel completely unable to compete with these women."[215]

Another woman confessed, "I have been excluded, isolated, barred from intimacy with him. I have lost someone who I thought was my best friend and most intimate companion in life."[216] (I should note at this point that men suffer similar feelings when their wives are addicted to porn.)

Dr. Norman Doidge describes his experience with men who preferred pornography to personal sexual interaction with their partners:

> They reported increasing difficulty in being turned
> on by their actual sexual partners, spouses or girlfriends,
> though they still considered them objectively attractive.
> When I asked if this phenomenon had any relationship
> to viewing pornography, they answered that it initially

helped them get more excited during sex but over time
had the opposite effect. Now, instead of using their senses
to enjoy being in bed, in the present, with their partners,
lovemaking increasingly required them to fantasize that
they were part of a porn script.[217]

I interviewed a woman who felt similar to Dr. Doidge's patients.
She told me:

> He is so consumed with that perfect image of what
> he's going after, that I'm not enough. And so, when we
> would have intimate time, it wasn't as good, because he
> had already been satisfied, his mind is someplace else.
> You're supposed to give to one another; it's a two-way
> street. And pornography takes you inward into a selfish
> path, and it just broke the intimate part of our marriage
> down.
>
> It cuts deep. It can really throw you for a whirl and
> make you feel insecure, for sure. I blamed myself; I
> wasn't meeting his needs somehow. He's looking [at porn]
> because he's not satisfied with me. When he can't even
> be intimate with you, you feel rejected, and so you begin
> to blame yourself. And, you know, well maybe I need to
> lose more weight. Maybe I need to dress up. Maybe I
> need to do this; maybe I need to do that. And it's never
> enough.[218]

Indeed, studies consistently show that internet pornography leads
to marital distress and destruction.[219] In fact, the emotional distance
created by pornography is often just as relationship-damaging as
non-virtual infidelity.[220] Perhaps that's why many men and women
consider online sexual activity a form of infidelity.[221]

Abandon Hope?

A study published in the *Journal of Adolescent Health* found that prolonged exposure to pornography led to the abandonment of the hope of sexual monogamy, and the acceptance of the belief that promiscuity is the natural state,[222] as well as a lack of attraction to family and child-raising.[223]

Other studies have shown that porn users see the institution of marriage as sexually confining.[224] What's more, their belief in the importance of marital faithfulness wanes, while their doubts about the value of marriage as a viable and essential social institution grow.[225]

In one survey, 62 percent of the United States' 1,600 top divorce and matrimonial attorneys reported that the internet was a significant factor in the divorces that they had handled during the past year. Of all the internet-related problems cited by the attorneys, an "obsessive interest" in online pornography was number two, playing a role in more than half (56 percent) of divorce cases.[226]

Porn's Social Toll

It's easy to see from this evidence that porn wreaks havoc on couples' relationships, but the damage doesn't stop there. When marriages fail, families are fractured and children are affected. Porn harms one of humanity's most vital institutions: the family.

Aristotle called the family "the association established by nature for the supply of mankind's everyday wants."[227] What happens within and to the family unit is significant because our families help us learn health concepts, social skills, and a value system. Strong families create healthy, functioning communities. Families help children develop into responsible citizens who contribute to society. As porn destroys marriages, families are divided, and divorce causes both short- and long-term harm.

A study published in the *American Sociological Review* (of 3,500 elementary-aged students) showed that children of divorce experienced setbacks in math and social skills and were more prone to feeling anxious, lonely, and sad, or tended to have low-self-esteem, compared with their peers whose parents remained married.[228]

Additionally, a 92-study meta-analysis on child well-being compared children living in divorced single-parent families with children living in intact (or two-parent) families. The data revealed that children of divorce scored lower than children in intact families across a variety of outcomes.[229]

The harms of divorce don't end there. A 15-country peer-reviewed study of Eastern and Western countries found that children of divorced parents face a higher risk of getting divorced themselves. The researchers found "substantial and highly statistically significant transmission effects in all samples,"[230] showing that the intergenerational transmission of divorce is a widespread phenomenon, with no exceptions. In other words, porn's effect on families can be multiplied across generations.

> "I am no longer sexually attractive or desirable to him. He's more attracted to the women depicted in his movies, magazines, and websites than he is to me, and I feel completely unable to compete with these women."
>
> ANONYMOUS message-board comment.

The "Porn Is Good for Relationships" Myth

Proponents of porn tout the notion that adult entertainment is somehow good for relationships, that it enhances a couple's sex life. One porn producer proudly told me:

> A guy goes home at night and his wife says, "Honey, you coming up to bed?" and he says, "I'm just gonna check the stock prices." He goes [to the computer], he looks at a couple naked women getting off, he whacks one off, he cleans up his mouse, he washes his hands off, climbs into bed, kisses his wife, and she turns over, they turn their separate ways, and they have a happy marriage.... I think porn has made for some very happy marriages and a lot of people aren't aware of that.[231]

Huffington Post author Stacey Nelkin has suggested that watching porn with your mate is "a good way to prevent cheating."[232] Not surprisingly, she provided no evidence to back up her claim.

And, in an issue of superstar Gwyneth Paltrow's online magazine, *Goop*, one of her nine sex tips was for couples to enhance their sex lives by watching porn.[233]

Given the vast evidence on the ways that porn harms intimate relationships, *Goop's* sex tip is akin to suggesting that eating ten pounds of butter daily will help you lose weight and lower your chances of acquiring heart disease.

Yes, the idea of porn enhancing sexual relationships is a popular notion on daytime talk shows and certain websites. Scientific evidence and real-life experience say otherwise.

It's time for a reality check: Porn is an ineffective and counterproductive solution to sexual boredom. It's a cheap substitute for the real work of improving a sexual relationship. Yes, sexual relationships can get stuck in ruts—the monotony of life can take its toll on any marriage. But offering porn as a solution? That's like offering heroin as a solution for boredom with life.

The story of porn injures intimate relationships. It feeds men and women lies about sexuality. It clouds what sex is about. It lies about how men should perform and what women truly desire and deserve. Boys and girls who grow up on porn sex turn into men and women who don't understand the nature of true intimacy. After all, porn sex is devoid of empathy, spirit, wisdom, mutuality, connectivity, exploration, joy, or true vulnerability. Because sex is such an integral part of intimate relationships, when it is derailed in such harmful ways there are serious consequences for our relationships.

As humans, we are physically and emotionally wired so that sex becomes the glue that helps hold a relationship together. It bonds us, creates trust, and keeps us anchored in our relationships. When porn invades our lives, it hijacks our sexuality by destroying the bond-building, intimate nature of sex. Porn takes sex from something that is revered and valued to something cheap and meaningless. From something vulnerable and mutually enjoyable to something aggressive, degrading, and abusing. Porn robs sexual intimacy of its care, connection, and commitment.

Porn sex is the antithesis of healthy sexuality. Porn is wrecking the intimacy, value, and bonding nature of sex, and it is also ravaging people's physical ability to have sex. After all, sexual intimacy is difficult when a man lacks the ability to have an erection.

10

THE END OF THE STORY:
Sexual Dysfunction

*"When Viagra was introduced ten years ago,
it would have been unusual to treat men in their thirties.
Now, however, it is common."*

—DR. JOHN DEAN, [234]

specialist in sexual medicine

Some apologists for porn claim that it makes a man sexually virile and enhances his sex life. In reality, porn is producing a generation of sexually disabled young men. They sit at the edge of their beds with limp penises. They are confused, frightened, and desperate for answers. Indeed, a global epidemic is hitting young men in their sexual primes. It's called "Porn-Induced Erectile Dysfunction" (PIED). [235] Men suffering from this disorder are flocking by the hundreds of thousands to support websites and message boards, begging for help. Here are a few typical accounts:

1. I am a 21-year-old man who *should* be in the prime of his sexual health. A couple of months ago, I entered into a new relationship with an absolutely amazing woman.

Everything was going great until it came to our first time being intimate. During foreplay, everything seemed to function as it should, then the "moment of truth" arrived. At that moment, all systems failed on my end. I went completely flaccid and couldn't get it up again. This is an incredibly humiliating experience, especially at my age.

This has happened one other time with this woman since then. There have been times when everything has worked fine, but it still seems incredibly difficult to maintain an erection. . . . At this point I have absolutely no confidence in the reliability of my own equipment, and, at only 21 years of age, this is incredibly frightening.

I have been to multiple doctors to address this issue. I am currently awaiting the results of a testosterone test, and I have an ultrasound next week, as well as a follow-up appointment with my urologist to . . . find a possible physical cause for this. I have tried all of the 'natural' remedies I can possibly think of. I've completely cut out all nicotine use, I have cut back on drinking, and I've tried taking L-arginine and horny goat weed. I even meditate to address any possible psychological causes. So far nothing has worked.

I admit I did watch a lot of porn, and some rather hardcore stuff at that. . . . I really am at my wit's end and am desperate to find a solution. I am young; this problem shouldn't even be on my radar, and I am terrified that this is going to be a lifelong issue.[236]

2. I've been dating my girlfriend for just over a year. For the first three months of our relationship, I never experienced an erection, even when she touched my penis while making out. In the fourth month of our relationship, I was finally able to get an erection and I lost my virginity to her. . . however, I found the sex to be extremely disappointing. I couldn't feel a thing with my penis. The only way I knew I was inside her was by sight. We had

sex many more times, and I couldn't orgasm. We would have sex for an hour or so until she asked if we could stop because she was tired.

About 5 months into our relationship, I unearthed a horrifying fact. I could cum during sex, but only if I fantasized about porn scenes I had seen in the past, or women other than my girlfriend engaging in extreme, porn-inspired sex with me. I can finally orgasm from sex, but the experience leaves a bitter taste in my mouth. Is this all sex is? Just masturbating with someone else's genitals instead of my hand? I don't want to believe that.

I feel guilty because I know my girlfriend feels sexually insufficient when I watch porn. If only she knew the truth, it would break her heart. I feel disappointed because I've never gotten to experience mind-blowing sex with a real person.... I need advice from people who have been in my shoes. If I stop masturbating and viewing porn, is there hope that I will ever have an amazing sex life?[237]

3. I am 37 years old and have been masturbating to porn since I was 15 or so. My addiction has gotten worse over the past few years, and I started viewing stuff I never thought I would have to, to get off.... Friday night my wife and I had sex (or tried) and I had ED [erectile dysfunction].... I thought it was from a muscle relaxer I had taken earlier that day for my back pain. So we tried again last night and same thing; it wouldn't get hard. I mean it wouldn't even think about getting hard. My wife doesn't know about my porn addiction, and I hope not to have to tell her! I blamed it on the muscle relaxers, but I didn't take one yesterday. She feels as though I don't find her attractive anymore; that's certainly not the problem! So I'm guessing I'm experiencing PIED? I never knew how much this stuff was really affecting me![238]

These comments highlight one of the dangers of getting trapped in porn's story. Looking at the same nude pictures or videos has diminishing arousal returns. Then we need something new and even more novel—more graphic, more extreme, more violent—just something markedly different. Our brains become conditioned to respond to only the most extreme content. Before long, sex in the real world just doesn't cut it anymore.

Thanks to neuroplasticity, our brains can change and heal. We can undo the damage that porn has caused.

That's why so many young men who start looking at porn in their tweens eventually lose the ability to be aroused by their real-life partners. That's when panic and sexual dysfunction can set in.

The MedHelp.org ED Forum has reported that 60 percent of 3,962 visitors seeking help for erectile dysfunction were younger than 25.[239]

In 2010, researchers at the University of Kansas discovered that 25 percent of college-age men in their study reported faking orgasms during sex because they couldn't reach climax.[240]

Today, more and more men under 30 are being prescribed Viagra and similar drugs, and experts have noted that the average age for men seeking ED prescriptions is falling steadily. Peter Baker, of the Men's Health Forum, stated that it is "well-known" among health professionals that younger men are turning to Viagra.[241]

A former porn producer admitted to knowing that porn causes erectile dysfunction at early ages. He said, "[F]rom a very early age, it [pornography] starts shaping the minds of these boys. . . . Boys that started looking at porn around 11 or 12 years old, which is the average age now, by the time that they're in their mid-20s, a quarter of them can't even get an erection in a real relationship anymore."[242]

In his 2018 Netflix comedy special, *Tambourine*, Chris Rock joked about the way his porn obsession affected him and his relationship with his now ex-wife. He said: "When you watch too much porn, you know what happens? You become, like, sexually autistic. You develop sexual autism. You have a hard time with eye contact and verbal cues. . . . You get desensitized. When you start watching porn, any porn will do. Then, later on . . . you need a perfect porn cocktail to get you off. I needed an Asian girl with a black girl's ass that speaks Spanish just to get my dick to move an inch." Often, jokes are funny because they resonate with a deeper truth.

PIED differs from age-related ED, which is usually caused by cardiovascular conditions or diabetes. Because of decreased blood flow or nerve dysfunction in the penis, men find it difficult to get and maintain an erection, as well as experience an orgasm.

For these twentysomethings, however, the problem is not physical dysfunction; it's a matter of sexual arousal in their brains. They have lost their sexual imaginations. Their brains are unable to function correctly because of sexual conditioning—their arousal has become connected to their porn use.

Dr. Norman Doidge says he began witnessing the emergence of PIED when the internet became accessible to the mainstream public. He worked with many men who were struggling to be turned on by their real-life sexual partners. These men stated that they experienced increased difficulty being turned on, even though they considered their partner to be sexually attractive. As we learned earlier, many of them found little enjoyment during sexual encounters, so they had to fantasize that they were a character in a porn script to experience pleasure.[243]

One newly married young man described his desperate situation in an online support group for men suffering from PIED:

I'm a twenty-five-year-old guy, recently married three months ago. Here's my story. I've been used to excessive porn and masturbation [for] ten years or so but never knew the consequences. As we all know, the more porn we watch, the kinkier we want it the next time. Now I've come to a stage where I don't like anything else other than cuckold* porn. I'm so addicted to it that I don't get erect at anything else. Even in bed with my wife, I get erect during foreplay but can't sustain it more than twenty to thirty seconds. It got me hooked so much that I've even talked to my wife about it to try this out in reality . . . which she obviously denied. I've gone online and talked to other men to convince them to realize my fantasy. I'm ashamed of myself, hugely. Yet I keep thinking of doing this again and again, such is my addiction.

I never knew doing all this will cause ED and make my mind do things which I never imagined, and I'm so devastated. Me and my wife had dreams for our new marriage, which are shattered at the moment. Our honeymoon was horrible due to the same reason. I've been in tears due to my condition. . . . So I need your help, guys. . . . Have I crossed the point of no return, or how much time will it take to get back to normal?[244]

The Science Behind the Porn/ED Connection

In 2011, Italian urologists conducted a survey of 28,000 internet pornography users, and their findings confirm the erectile dysfunction/pornography-use connection. When interviewed about the survey, urologist Carlo Foresta, head of the Italian Society of Andrology and Sexual Medicine and professor at the University of Padua, noted that the findings were not surprising. Indeed, 70 percent

---

* "Cuckold" describes the fetish of men who find masochistic pleasure in watching their wives have sex with other men. The man is complicit in the infidelity and often helps arrange the meetings.

of the young men he treated for ED at his clinic were heavy users of internet porn.

According to the survey, many subjects began "excessive consumption" of pornography at age 14 or younger. By the time they hit their mid-20s, they used porn daily—becoming desensitized to "even the most violent" images. Foresta concluded that developing one's sexuality in the virtual world, absent real-life relationships, caused a gradual, but "devastating" result.[245]

Researchers theorize that the main cause of PIED is sexual conditioning that results in low dopamine levels. (Dopamine, as we learned earlier, is a driving force behind our physical pleasure.) There are two types of PIED. Chronic PIED results from continual overstimulation. Situational PIED affects a man when his dopamine levels plummet because his real-life sex differs from his porn-inspired expectations.

For many porn users, low dopamine levels result in the inability to achieve an erection. So they need constant "hits" of porn to become excited.

Author Gary Wilson, whom we met in Chapter 1, explains what is medically going on when this happens. (Take a breath, because this gets a little technical.)

> Normally, dopamine-producing nerve cells in the reward circuitry activate the sexual [libido] centers of the hypothalamus, which in turn activate the erection centers in the spinal cord, which send nerve impulses to the genitalia. A steady stream of nerve impulses, which release nitric oxide into the penis and its blood vessels, maintain an erection. Nitric oxide, in turn, stimulates the blood-vessel dilator cGMP, the on/off switch for engorgement and erection. The more cGMP that is available, the more durable the erection.

Erections start with dopamine and end with cGMP.
Sexual enhancement drugs work by halting the breakdown of cGMP and allowing it to accumulate in the penis.
But if the patient's brain isn't producing enough pleasure
signals, ED drugs will not increase libido or pleasure even
if they can produce an erection."[246]

Today, given the proliferation of internet porn, overstimulation
of the brain's reward circuitry system is easy and quick to achieve.
Imagine the implications for a young male who has spent a decade
or more overstimulating his brain before having his first real-life
sexual experience.

Like the proverbial frog in a pot of slow-heating water, the young
man slowly (and without his awareness) loses the dopamine sensitivity his brain needs for normal, face-to-face sexual interaction.
He panics when he is unable to achieve an erection in real life. In
desperation, he brings porn into the bedroom, or he mentally dis-
engages during sex, turning to his favorite (and most intense) porn
scenes in a desperate attempt to get the dopamine hits he requires.
His partner has ceased to matter to him.

As one porn consumer I interviewed told me:

"I fell in love with my girlfriend about two years ago,
and I realized I couldn't get aroused to save my life . . .
because I compared [her] to the fantasy, the real thing
just didn't work. And it was the first time I came to understand that this porn thing affected me. . . . The rush wasn't
there. So it affected me socially, the way I viewed relationships . . . and then when I actually found I was in a
relationship, I couldn't produce [arousal] in an intimate
environment."[247]

Indeed, porn is stunting us emotionally, ravaging us physically,
and destroying some of the most intimate, beautiful, and valuable

THE END OF THE STORY: Sexual Dysfunction

parts of our lives. It has hijacked our sexuality, throwing us so far off course that it is hard to find the path to recovery. But there is a path that can bring us healing and wholeness.

Quitting Makes a Difference

Here's some good news: Those who work with men suffering from the negative consequences of porn use (including addiction and PIED) have discovered that porn's effects can be reversed, over time.

(I should note here that porn-induced sexual dysfunction is not limited to men. Many women struggle to experience sexual pleasure—in real life, with real people—without the aid of porn.)

Thanks to neuroplasticity, our brains can change and heal. We can undo the damage that porn has caused. Here are a few testimonials, gleaned from surveys and online message boards:

> "I am a living example. First when I started NoFap,*
> I [had] PIED. Now it's like seventy percent cured, just in
> forty-one days of abstaining from P[orn] and M[asturba-
> tion]. Plus I got my first wet dream during the process, as
> well as morning erections are back every day."[248]

> "I am proud of living without PMO [porn mastur-
> bation orgasm] for two weeks. I'm single but I rely on
> friends, family, yoga, massage, exercise, and breathing
> to get by each day. I am learning many natural ways of
> relaxing and coping with my brain and environment. I'm
> more relaxed, generous, and appreciative with people.
> However, I feel great pain, lethargy, apathy, sadness,
> frustration and loneliness sometimes. The frequency and
> duration of my time in the pits is definitely decreasing.

---

* "Fap" is internet slang for masturbation to porn. "NoFap" means abstaining from it.

There's a lot of comfort remembering that, whenever my dopamine needle drops real low. One problem with improvement is that we forget how messed up we were when we started. LOL."[249]

"It's strange but this is the second time I've gone over two months and this time I feel like I can go on forever. My libido comes and goes but I definitely know it's there if I need it. Porn ultimately has no value. I don't consider going back all that much, although the thought comes back from time to time. I think of it like smoking. Would I try one cigarette after years of quitting, just to see if I am still addicted? Of course not. Porn isn't all that much different. Those neuron pathways are so strong that one image can send you back to bingeing."[250]

"If you can manage at least 3 weeks, you'll see how powerful all of this is. The clarity and lack of depression for me was extremely noticeable, and you will likely feel like a different person. It gave me some hope that there is nothing fundamentally wrong with me. Just having that experience of clarity and lack of depression can be a powerful thing. It's worth it, but it can take a while to get the hang of it."[251]

Yes, recovery from porn addiction can be a difficult journey. Wilson has noted that "quitting porn" can cause dramatic withdrawal symptoms, such as an initial "dramatic temporary drop in libido," as well as "insomnia, irritability, panic, despair, concentration problems, and even flu-like symptoms." He says that, in most cases, the recovery period lasts three weeks. However, he found that the earlier one's porn use starts, the longer it takes to recover. Some men require up to two years to make meaningful and lasting progress.[252]

Recovery, Wilson adds, centers on completely avoiding the extreme stimulation of internet pornography. Going "cold turkey" helps to "rewire" one's brain, getting the chemicals under control. That's when people can break free from chronic porn use and its detrimental effects. And that process is the focus of this book's next section.

SECTION TWO

11

FINDING PERSONAL FREEDOM:
Framing the Struggle and Overcoming Shame

"Healing is the journey. The destination is yourself."

—PHILIP BERK[253]

Humans desire freedom; it's in our nature. People throughout history have been willing to fight and die for their freedom. When we are free, we have the personal autonomy to make choices and control our lives. Autonomy goes hand in hand with freedom. Addiction does not.

Addiction robs us of health, happiness, integrity, and dignity. We begin to feel out of control, as if our brains (and lives) have been taken over by a seemingly irresistible force. For many people, this force comes in the form of compulsive porn use.

Fortunately, addiction to porn is not a life sentence. We can find personal freedom from pornography, just as we can from any addiction. But while this freedom is possible, it's not easy. Freedom from porn involves a struggle, the struggle to rewire our minds and reclaim our autonomy. Picture it this way: If porn has carjacked the vehicle called your life, the only solution is to remove the carjacker from the driver's seat.

At this point in the book, I hope you have come to appreciate the damage porn causes and the danger it represents. If porn has been a problem in your life, you want to break free from it. Or you want to help and/or protect others who are being affected by porn. But how?

To help us answer that question, I have reviewed decades' worth of research on overcoming addiction. I have spoken with leading experts in the fields of neuroscience and psychology. And I have conducted extensive interviews with a variety of people who have found freedom from porn addiction. In the following pages, I will share what I have learned about porn addiction and what it takes to overcome it.

Acknowledging the Problem and Framing the Struggle

The first step toward change is admitting that change is necessary to fix a problem or conquer a challenge. Those struggling with porn must be honest enough to admit their need for help and healing. But this self-awareness is only the first step. The way we define and frame a problem is crucial.

Many people regard overcoming porn use as a moral struggle. The porn addict is a moral failure, or a "sinner."

I acknowledge that porn addiction can result from flawed morals. However, labeling its victims as evil is not helpful. Such labels place people in a box, a prison cell of unhealthy shame. And a person who feels shamed and humiliated is unlikely to seek help. He or she is more likely to withdraw, to hide. Often, this leads to more porn use and a deeper addiction.

Counselors, psychologists, and others have achieved positive results by striving to understand porn in the larger context of addictions. They realize that, like other addictions, this one is a complex emotional, psychological, and neurological struggle. This approach is more helpful, accurate, and compassionate than judging or ridiculing someone. That's why it provides a realistic path to freedom.

Those who battle compulsivity and addiction need to understand that they are not evil, and not alone. They are part of a larger culture of addiction.

As psychologist, author, and sexual-addiction expert Dan Allender explains, "Just as a fish is unaware of the water that sets the parameters of its world, so we often fail to take in the milieu in which we live."[254]

Yes, our modern high-speed, media-saturated culture is overstimulated, overstressed, overcrowded, and overconnected. And yet many of us feel more isolated than ever. We grow up in a world steeped in consumerism and the quick fix. Our "drive-through" mentality doesn't allow us room to process stress, pain, depression, loneliness, and all the other challenges that drive us to the temporary salve that addictions provide. In order to squelch feelings of anxiety, emptiness, and unhappiness, many try to cope via excessive and compulsive drug and alcohol use, shopping, work, eating, gambling, gaming, sex, and/or escaping to the fantasy world of pornography.

Allender calls these compulsions or addictions an "endless array of escape-ruin opportunities."[255]

> "The thing that hurts most about my experience in the adult industry is seeing how human beings can treat another human being like they're not even worth the ground they walk on. That you mean nothing."
>
> TANYA B., former porn performer

Here's how actor and author Russell Brand explained his experience with porn and sex addiction: "If I make sex the panacea, the salve to this pain . . . I will soon lose control of my sexual conduct and I'll end up in more pain."[256]

Whatever the source of one's addiction, the addictive object or force (the bottle of wine, the extra-large dessert, or the porn video) ultimately mocks us with the reality that we are still empty, alone, and feeling even more pain and shame. It's hard to break free from the indulge/shame/repeat cycle, because compulsions and addictions are great deceivers. Dr. Harvey Schwartz, a clinical psychologist, psychotherapist, and consultant, explains that addictions allow many people to experience a kind of "false freedom" from pain, worry, loneliness, and stress—especially in the early stages. But then comes the "diabolical reversal" as addictions take us hostage while we imagine they are freeing us.[257] In other words, porn promises a shortcut to happiness, but it corrupts our minds and demeans us in the process.

Removing the Facade

Compulsive consumers of porn are drawn to a fantasy world that helps them hide from the pain in their lives. A young man might feel frustrated and rejected in his actual romantic life, but in Porn Universe, he is desired by thousands of beautiful and sexually available women. Those smiles and moans of pleasure are just for him. His insecurity, doubt, and awkwardness have been replaced by confidence and sexual prowess.

But what happens when his fantasy and reality collide?

When a person cuts through porn's cover story, the facade is exposed. The fantasy is ruined. Part of porn's illusion is its picture of what "good sex" looks like when it comes to male and female needs, arousal patterns, and sexual performance.

What's more, porn promotes the myth that its on-screen sexual encounters are voluntary, safe, and enjoyable for the performers. (We've already learned this is false, from several first-person accounts.) Beyond that, porn tells the viewer, "You're in control here. These women are performing for your personal enjoyment."

This is why learning the truth about the porn industry, how it operates, and what the actors and actresses really experience—or don't experience—is crucial to disrupting porn's powerful allure. Once we come face-to-face with the truth, porn's fantasy becomes impotent; it loses its power over us.

Indeed, after seeing our film *Raised on Porn*, which is a companion to this book, 93 percent of viewers said this documentary inspired them to be more proactive in protecting their children from porn. To date, millions of people have viewed *Raised on Porn*, which presents facts on the porn industry, interviews with those affected by porn, and insights from mental health professionals—just like this book.

The book and the film present the cold truth that porn doesn't represent a harmless fantasy. Porn, like prostitution, involves real people who are violently degraded and dehumanized.

Tanya, the former porn performer we met in Chapter 4, told me, "The thing that hurts the most about my experience in the adult industry is seeing how human beings can treat another human like they're not even worth the ground that they walk on. That you're non-existent; you mean nothing. How someone can be so inhumane and not worry about a person's feelings, their health, is an extreme thing because I was lucky, only being ripped, and [getting] sick, and [getting] pink eye. I've had friends that I had to go and get after their scene was done and take them to the hospital because their insides were falling out of their anal cavity. And the producers don't care. You finish the scene, then you can do whatever you need to do."

She concluded, "You're lucky if you're even a number. You're just a body that's there to make them dollars. . . . And if you don't move fast enough, they'll move somebody else in."[258]

Not long after this interview, Tanya tried to commit suicide because of her inner turmoil. Thankfully, she survived, but stories like hers make it clear that porn is inflicting real harm on its performers, and on its consumers—many of whom are children and adolescents.

Hope for Recovery

Consumers who are addicted to porn understand that freedom isn't a simple matter of summoning more willpower. Although willpower is an essential step to gaining freedom, addiction is more complex than this one aspect. Addiction sinks its roots deep into the mind and body. The struggle to overcome porn addiction is neurological and neuropsychological. It's a battle fought in the synapses of our brains, and in the chemicals flowing through our bodies. Porn, like alcohol or drugs, causes changes in the brain, changes that must be addressed and treated.

The good news is that porn's effects on our brains are reversible.

Gabe Deem is the founder and director of Reboot Nation, an organization that is dedicated to helping people overcome compulsive porn use. Deem overcame his own porn addiction and is helping thousands of others along the same path.

He says that helping victims understand the brain science behind their addiction is crucial for success. Once a person struggling with a porn addiction understands how visual stimuli affect the brain, he or she can follow a road map to recovery.

The concept of neuroplasticity is an empowering concept to grasp for those struggling with compulsive porn use, because it enables them to grasp the potential for change. As we discussed earlier in the book, neuroplasticity refers to the way that the brain can change by linking neurons together into certain pathways and networks. Neuro refers to the brain, and plasticity refers to the brain's ability to change or be molded, just like plastic. The important point to understand here is that your brain can literally be changed by porn-use habits.

The good news is that plastic can bend both ways. That means we have the potential to change our habits and deprogram and rewire our brains by adopting new, healthy behaviors and ways of thinking—as we disrupt and replace the unhealthy ones.

In other words, if one repeats positive behaviors and ways of thinking enough, and avoids the negative ones, he or she has the potential to build new pathways and new patterns in the brain, as well as lay down new circuitry—so that the brain, the personality, and the behaviors interact and mutually reinforce one another. This symbiotic relationship among positive behaviors, thinking, and emotions enables new patterns and circuits to develop in the brain. It's how neuroplasticity can ultimately work in your favor.

Neuroplasticity is a process of observation, access, disruption, and replacement. It's activated by forming new habits. Learning how to activate one's neuroplasticity is the essence of healing the brain. Once habits and their neurological correlates are disrupted (and neuroplasticity potentials are activated), new circuitry can be laid down in a variety of ways, including prayer, meditation, yoga, journaling, exercise, spending time in nature, etc.[259]

By retraining and rewiring the brain, a person can make significant progress on the journey toward freedom from porn. Along the way, those hormones and brain chemicals will find a place of healthy balance. Framing one's struggle with porn this way can provide the mental and emotional fortitude to move forward with confidence, because hope is on the horizon. The neurological lens for understanding and framing compulsive porn use is helpful to all involved. We know that porn use and many other addictive behaviors have emotional, behavioral, psychological, and neurological components. It is important for all of them to be addressed.

When you are inside of an elaborate corn maze, for example, the endless turns can feel maddening. However, if you could "zoom out" and see things from a distance, you could map your exit plan. In a similar way, understanding the neurological aspect of the battle against compulsive porn use gives a person that bird's-eye view. If we can understand how our brains got trapped or became hostage to addiction, we can learn how to escape.

The Importance of "Self-Compassion"

Unhealthy shame is an enemy of freedom. It significantly inhibits one's progress toward overcoming any addiction. Such shame can make us feel worthless and hopeless. On the other hand, healthy shame activates one's conscience and helps a person realize, "My behavior is not matching my personal convictions." This form of shame is non-condemning and not excessively harsh. Best of all, it activates a behavioral change to rectify the feelings of discomfort, anxiety, and inner turmoil.[260]

Healthy shame says, "I am doing something bad, and I know I am better than this. I can change."

Unhealthy shame says, "I am doing something bad because I *am* bad and I can't change." Unhealthy shame perpetuates this destructive cycle: I am bad → I do bad → I do bad → I am bad.

Healthy shame says: I have done bad → I am not bad → I can stop doing bad because I am not bad.

Dr. Schwartz notes that "one of the common struggles of all addictions is the battle with shame. Many addicts deal with their shame via denial, blame, and/or rationalization." Sometimes, Schwartz explains, they drown themselves in self-pity and self-hatred, but this only reinforces the need for more addictive behavior, "welcoming the numbing and escaping aspects of the addiction to neutralize shame, often with an 'I don't care' cover narrative."[261]

For example, Gene McConnell spent years struggling with an intense porn and sex addiction that started when he was a child. Today, however, he has overcome that addiction and leads an organization helping men conquer similar struggles. Here's how he describes unhealthy shame: "Based on my personal experience and the experience of so many men that I have helped along the way, I have seen that shame is one of the greatest barriers to bringing about change. Shame is a belief about oneself as being defective, inadequate, unworthy, and unlovable. Shame says that whatever bad things they have done or have happened to them, it is because they are bad. This feeling keeps many porn consumers stuck . . . because they feel that they can't get help. As long as the shadow of shame is looming, everything stays in the dark."[262]

The process of disrupting the toxic power of unhealthy shame is central to overcoming addiction, because shame is an incredibly debilitating, devastating, and disempowering emotion. After 30-plus years of treating men and women who have experienced sexual trauma, sexual addictions, and other forms of sexual brokenness, Dr. Dan Allender observed that "the experience of shame sends a shudder so deep through the soul that most human beings would rather disappear, lie, or give up all that feels dear to escape the cataclysm. . . . Shame makes a person mad, if not insane, and is the impetus for some of the most harmful acts against other human beings."

Shame, adds Allender, "demands hiding and isolation," because "[e]xposure intensifies the volcanic meltdown of the self, fragmenting, sluicing, and congealing the exposed parts in a frozen mess."[263]

Because it is so harmful, we know that unhealthy shame is one of the most important emotions to address on the journey toward healing. Only when unhealthy shame is exposed and confronted can the problems of addiction, compulsion, and sexual trauma emerge from their dark corners and into the light of day, where real help and healing can take place.

On a practical level, one of the most effective things a person can do to unseat the power of unhealthy shame is to have compassion for him- or herself. This paradigm shift recognizes vulnerability to addiction. Such compassion allows people to separate who they are from their destructive behaviors. They then begin to appreciate the size of their struggle and the limits of human weakness. This helps them develop true self-compassion. They no longer want to shame or condemn themselves; they want to overcome their problems. Instead of carrying the burdens of helplessness, anger, and hostility, they find a more affirming and empowered place, one built on tenderness, humility, vulnerability, and compassion.

Dr. Kristin Neff, a pioneer in the empirical study of self-compassion, explains:

> Compassion is concerned with the alleviation of suffering. When we feel compassion for our own pain—especially when the pain comes from our maladaptive habits and behaviors—we want to heal our pain. We want to make changes and improvements that will help us suffer less. While the motivational power of self-criticism comes from fear of self-punishment, the motivational power of self-compassion comes from the desire to be healthy.
>
> Self-compassion recognizes that failure is not only inevitable, but it's also our best teacher, something to be explored rather than avoided at all costs. Self-compassion

also allows us to acknowledge areas of personal weakness by recognizing that imperfection is part of the shared human experience. We can then work on improving ourselves, not because we're unacceptable as we are, but because we want to thrive and be happy.[264]

One effective strategy for cultivating self-compassion is the exercise of compassionate witnessing—going back in time and communicating with the person who was first exposed to porn and bearing witness to what happened in the heart and mind.

Most people struggling with a porn addiction were first exposed to porn during their youth, making them feel disturbed, titillated, nauseated, fascinated, scared, confused, threatened, amused, or a host of other emotions. And children often lack the ability to make sense of what is happening to them. As we learned earlier, the brain's frontal cortex (responsible for reasoning, critical thinking, and decision-making) isn't fully developed until one's mid-20s.

So, when children or adolescents are exposed to porn, they lack the cognitive capacities to analyze what is happening to them, or to use reason to decide whether to continue consumption. Simply put, they are overwhelmed. They are victims of their exposure.

Compassionate witnessing means going back to that younger version of oneself (who first faced these images) and feeling empathy. Compassionate witnessing can help a person heal emotionally.

Compassionate witnessing involves getting into a quiet and meditative state; releasing distracting thoughts; relaxing the body; and taking a few long, slow breaths. This allows us to "meet" our younger self at the place and time of the exposure. That's when an inner dialogue can begin.

For example, one could say, "I am so sorry that you were exposed to these images and that there were no protections to safeguard your heart and mind from this destructive force. I am sorry there wasn't an adult figure there to protect you. I am sorry for the distortion of ideas and outlook that you were indoctrinated with through exposure to those images, and how it all affected the trajectory of your life."

Apologizing to the younger self can help cultivate compassion in one's heart. It can also foster a sense of healing from the trauma of that early exposure.

The mental exercise of visiting with one's younger self can be expanded from apologizing, witnessing, and recognizing to remembering specific early exposures to pornography and gaining access to the messages that were downloaded into the mind. One can do this by remembering oneself at the time of each event, recalling the meanings and messages that were implanted in the mind, and then replacing those toxic messages with more compassionate, healthy, and truthful messages. This powerful exercise of replacing deception with truth is vital to the healing process.

This exercise can also include grieving. Being able to grieve what happened to the younger self who was exposed to pornography is a powerful-yet-tender way to cultivate self-compassion. Entering into grief moves people from self-loathing, shame, and guilt to a realization of what they have suffered—the corrosion of their integrity and dignity, the unhealthy behaviors, the missed opportunities, and more.

To be clear, I am advocating for self-compassion to replace unhealthy shame. However, that doesn't mean we are not responsible for our actions. After all, compassion and responsibility are not mutually exclusive. They are complementary. Self-compassion gives us a healthy general sense of responsibility and motivates us to fulfill our specific responsibilities.

When we view our struggle through the lens of self-compassion, we realize that our identity isn't chained to things that happened to us or our mistakes, especially the mistakes that don't represent who we truly are. Self-compassion is not self-pity. It's not a victim mentality. Rather, it replaces the heavy burden of unhealthy shame, self-loathing, anger, and hatred with understanding, compassion, affirmation, and empowerment.

Our humanity is flawed yet beautiful, imperfect but worthy of appreciation. Self-compassion and healthy self-love enable us to embrace ourselves (and others), flaws and all. We realize that we all have more potential than a past failure might indicate. This realization enables us to honestly address and confront our mistakes and how they have hurt us and others.

Conversely, self-condemnation, unhealthy shame, and rigid dogmatism tie a person to his failures, holding back the river of healing that is available through self-compassion and healthy self-love.

That's why self-compassion is the better option. It's a transformative process that removes toxic beliefs and emotions so that healing and hope can flow into one's life.

12

FINDING PERSONAL FREEDOM:
Building Your Plan for Recovery

Successful recovery from addiction doesn't happen by accident. It takes planning, commitment, resolve, and endurance. That's why creating a clear and measurable action plan is vital. The following pages contain practical wisdom gathered from experts who have helped many people break free from porn addiction.

I hope the advice you are about to read will help you or someone you know find freedom from porn addiction.

Move Beyond Denial, Resolve to Resist, and Believe Freedom Is Possible

The first step on the path toward freedom from porn is admitting that there is a problem. This means moving past denial. Denial can take various forms. Some people minimize the problem: "I don't watch porn that much, and I don't watch the really hardcore stuff."

Others rationalize: "I know porn can be harmful, but I'm feeling lonely and rejected right now."

And then there is flat-out repudiation: "I know I watch porn a lot, but it's not hurting me, and it's not affecting anyone else! Besides, this is a free country, isn't it?"

To find freedom from porn, strive to avoid any form of denial, and move to a place of humility and self-awareness. Only then can we admit the need for help and restoration.

Next, resolve to resist looking at porn. This resoluteness is vital. Others may be angry at you for your porn habit—and desperate for you to quit. However, you can't stop until you truly want to stop. You can't outsource resolve. As one recovered porn user told me (anonymously), "The first step to quitting porn is you really have to want to quit porn. You need to be sick and tired of porn, and the sickness that it causes you, in order to quit."

Part of generating the resolve to stop using porn is facing its destructive and addictive powers. That's why it needs to be rooted out of your life, for good.

I hope what you have read so far has given you a better understanding of how quitting porn is difficult, but absolutely possible!

As part of building a "freedom from porn" plan, I recommend creating a list of reasons for quitting porn. Write them down somewhere. Memorize them. Keep them ever-present.

Here are a few examples of compelling and specific reasons:

"Porn is diminishing my sense of self."

"Porn is robbing me of the ability to interact with the opposite sex in a healthy way."

"Porn has caused me to have a dysfunctional sexuality with my spouse."

"Porn is wasting way too much of my time."

"Porn perpetuates the sexual abuse and exploitation of women and children, and I don't want to be a part of that. I don't want to support that."

As these examples indicate, one's reasons for quitting can be personal, philosophical, or both. The key is that the reasons matter. When we are deeply invested in our reasons, they provide courage and the strength of conviction, especially when temptation is strong. Of course, believing "I need to change!" is not enough. You must also believe that you *can* change. This is where hope enters the picture. Hope is the powerful force that allows us to believe that things don't always have to be the way they are right now. Change is possible!

Dan Allender eloquently explains how hope brings change and freedom: "Hope refuses to believe that the inevitable is so. What has always been and can't change is an illusion; if anything is true, it is that change is inevitable, not that the inevitable will not change."[265]

He adds, "Hope demands that we challenge our habitual reenactment with boldness, honesty, and kindness. This is counterintuitive. But we will not regain the ground of hope by force or mere self-control. No addict has changed merely because of the pain."[266]

Indeed, pain alone doesn't push us toward success. Hope must be present. Hope is powerful enough to overcome pain. Harvard Medical School professor and *New Yorker* staff writer Dr. Jerome Groopman writes in his book *The Anatomy of Hope*, "Researchers are learning that a change in mind-set has the power to alter neurochemistry. Belief and expectation—the key elements of hope—can block pain by releasing the brain's endorphins and enkephalins, mimicking the effects of morphine."[267]

In other words, acquiring a sense of hope about your situation can alleviate pain, enabling you to move forward despite withdrawal, discomfort, and other challenges. Some of you may feel so worn down by failure that hope seems like a distant light—something out of reach.

Robert L. Leahy, PhD, is the director of the American Institute for Cognitive Therapy and a clinical professor of psychology at Weill-Cornell Medical School. He says that one way to cultivate hope when you feel utterly hopeless is to live in the moment. He advises: "Stop and think about what is happening right now. Is this moment hopeless? Sit quietly, noticing your breath, letting it in and out, watching it come and go. Feel your feet against the floor. Hear the sounds around you. Peel an orange and smell the tang within. Listen to the music and feel the notes run through you. The present is here, every moment, every day. When the future is gone and you live fully alive here and now, you put an end to hopelessness."[268]

Henri Nouwen, philosopher and theologian, suggests an alternate path. He says not to worry that things are not okay right now, because hope is a belief in things that are out of reach—things not yet seen or realized. He encourages those feeling hopeless to keep persevering, saying, "Hope means to keep living amid desperation and to keep humming in the darkness."[269]

Commit to Transparency

As noted earlier, understanding that you are not alone on this journey is a critical element in overcoming addiction. The resolve to quit porn can be strengthened immensely by including others in the struggle and in the plans. The willingness to communicate with a trusted person is a great sign that someone truly wants to change.

Dr. Kevin Skinner, psychologist, author, and expert in porn addiction recovery, believes that when people take the courageous first step of being vulnerable by seeking outside help, they are moving toward real and lasting change. Sharing problematic behavior with another person brings matters into the light. And it can relieve internal turmoil, turmoil that often results in relapses or setbacks.[270]

A critical step toward maintaining transparency is joining a support group or an online community where you can share experiences, struggles, strategies, and questions with an understanding and empathic group.

The battle with addiction often consumes much of a person's emotional strength and headspace, but it's a battle most of us feel uncomfortable sharing. However, if you can find a community support system, it will dispel feelings of loneliness and isolation. This is important because loneliness is an enemy of recovery and healing; it is the alienating sensation of feeling unwanted, unloved, and unlovable. Extreme loneliness carries the risk of mental illness, or an even deeper level of addiction.

If you or someone you know has struggled to find an in-person support group, I recommend the Fortify online platform and app. (Visit joinfortify.com for more information.)

Thousands of people (men and women) who struggle with porn use have found freedom via the Fortify program. Other helpful online communities can be found at rebootnation.org and nofap.com.

Find an Accountability Partner

Addiction-recovery experts agree that having an accountability partner is an indispensable part of the journey to freedom. This partner can be a trusted friend, family member, spiritual leader, or anyone who can understand the struggle and be available when needed.

An accountability partner can remind you of the reasons you decided to free yourself from porn in the first place—and can be there for you when you need one-on-one support.

Your accountability partner should truly want you to succeed, care about your well-being, and provide support when the journey becomes difficult. When shame comes flooding in, your accountability partner can help you re-center and remind you of your true identity. When you are tempted, he or she can provide many reasons to stay strong.

Find a Therapist

Many people find it embarrassing to seek a therapist. Even those who acknowledge the benefits of therapy for other people resist putting themselves in the vulnerability of the therapist's chair.

Seeing a therapist takes courage, conviction, humility, and transparency. It exposes our vulnerability and our desire to solve our problems by ourselves. The decision can be especially difficult for men, because we are socialized to believe that vulnerability is weakness. In truth, vulnerability and transparency require strength. Only when we are honest with ourselves can we set a course for maturity, healing, and transformation.

If you struggle with the idea of therapy, consider this: If we have a medical problem, such as illness or injury, we seek a medical professional. If we face a legal challenge, we search for a well-qualified and experienced lawyer. Why should it be any different with our psychological and emotional health? There are professionals who have spent most of their lives helping people overcome porn-related addictions and trauma. They can help you on your journey.

A skilled therapist can identify areas of pain, trauma, emotional congestion, confusion, etc., and then skillfully help you navigate a path of healing and wholeness.

Therapists can take the broken parts of our lives and help us put them back together. If you feel alienated, a therapist can help you discover a place of belonging. If you suffer from shame, a therapist can help you recover your human dignity. Therapy can help you break free from addiction and become a whole, healthy, and thriving human being.

Of course, it's important to find the right therapist. Your search might end with therapist number one, or number ten. It might require a few initial consultations to find someone you are comfortable with.

One key factor to consider is feedback. Therapy should be a two-way street. If you are sharing your deepest struggles, your therapist should respond with insight and wisdom. A good therapist should help you gain new perspectives and create a road map to navigate your emotions. If you are the only one who talks during a therapy session, you should move on. Yes, a therapist should be a good listener, but he or she should provide insight and direction as well.

I realize that therapy can be expensive, but how much is an investment in overcoming a harmful addiction worth?

And many places, especially college towns, offer low-cost therapy. Another option for accessible and affordable therapy is via the Rtribe website (rtribe.org) and app. At Rtribe you can access affordable and anonymous professional therapy and coaching from experts who are familiar with the struggles of porn addiction.

Building a Fortress of Truth

Porn is not just a set of images; it's an intricate system of exploitation—a system of mass influence, mass marketing, and, in many ways, mass abuse that leads to more abuse. Porn is also a lie. It is a lie about what sex is supposed to be like. It is a lie about what it means to be masculine and feminine.

Porn can't cure your loneliness or feelings of inadequacy, depression, or rejection. It won't enhance your sex life, or your partner's. Those smiling women on the screen are not truly enjoying what they are experiencing. (I have interviewed many porn performers about this, and you have read some of their comments in this book.)

It is a lie that a male actor's erection is due to true feelings of love and passion for his partner. And it's a lie that porn is consequence-free. It makes an impact—physically, emotionally, and relationally.

Reflect on what you have learned about the porn story's lies. Have you been manipulated into believing some of them? Is that why you are trapped in a destructive cycle?

Recovery from porn involves education and re-education, programming and deprogramming. Discovering the truth about porn will tear down the mental fantasy—the fantasy that keeps you wanting more porn, including porn that is increasingly violent and extreme.

For example, a man might believe the fantasy that porn actresses truly enjoy the kind of sex they are having. But when he reads interviews with these women and learns about the physical pain and injury, the deception and manipulation, and the emotional and psychological turmoil, he realizes that he has been sold a lie. This realization becomes a tool to combat the next urge to consume porn.

> Porn cultivates a demand for commercial sex, and that demand is why sex trafficking flourishes around the globe. Recognizing that porn use is perpetuating the harm of vulnerable young women can dismantle its erotic fantasy.

If you are struggling with porn, it's important to understand that the Porn Universe is an exploitative system. This truth should strike a chord in your heart, your spirit. It should awaken your sense of integrity and dignity. You can contrast the fantasies and deception with the truth. This might create inner turmoil, because that's what happens when our actions conflict with our core beliefs. But once your values align with your behavior, rejecting the porn system becomes organic. It feels natural and healthy.

Once you have replaced fantasy with correct beliefs (lies with truth), then you will have a new framework for understanding porn's role in your life. You will stand on a firm moral and ethical foundation. Here's a comparison many people find helpful: Research has shown that a college student's attitude toward drinking is the best predictor of a future alcohol problem. If a student believes that it's okay to binge-drink occasionally, he is far more likely to engage in this behavior.[271]

Likewise, our attitudes about sexuality, intimacy, and ethics are strong predictors of whether or not we will fall prey to porn addiction. If we value human dignity, equality, and the right to live free of oppression and violence—if we value childhood innocence and meaningful adult intimacy—we should reject the porn system. Addiction expert Dr. Stanton Peele explains:

> Values are important to all addictions. . . . To say that your values influence your desire and ability to fight addiction is to say that you act in line with what you believe in and what you care about. Such values can be remarkably potent. . . . As a society, and as individuals, we need to grasp that there is no more important facilitator or antidote to addiction than our values. If you have these values, they help you to fight addiction. And if you don't, developing such values is potentially a critical therapeutic tool."[272]

Although cultivating values that oppose porn consumption is an important tool, building a defense against porn requires more than one tool. I've encountered people whose beliefs and values don't support porn use, but they still can't stop. They live in a constant and painful state of cognitive dissonance, where beliefs and behavior are at war.

Here's why: While our value system is a very important tool, a person might continue his porn habit—even if it clashes with his values—if he doesn't believe porn is harming him or any of the people he loves. (Compare this scenario to a person addicted to junk food. He knows this stuff isn't healthy and that there are better options available. But it doesn't seem to be harming him. Plus, a lot of his friends eat junk food, and they seem to be doing okay. Until they aren't.)

Dealing with Withdrawal

Withdrawal is another reason people struggle with breaking their addiction to porn. In fact, many aren't aware that breaking the porn habit creates withdrawal, so they are unprepared. That's why developing withdrawal strategies and skills is another important tool in the toolbox. It is important to understand that withdrawal might happen and to be prepared for it. Being prepared is vital to staying on the path to freedom.

In his book *Cutting It Off: Breaking Porn Addiction and How to Quit for Good*, former porn addict J. S. Park reveals that his withdrawal involved "the shakes, sweating, reduced concentration, foggy thinking, a sudden flood of sexual images, insomnia, and an 'itchy' anxiety." He adds that the withdrawal period can last weeks, even months, explaining:

> Perhaps the very worst of these [symptoms] is the acute onset of sexual imagery in your head, usually with zero warning or external cause. Since your brain is so familiar with easy online access, there will be a time when your neurons are almost gasping for porn. Any smoker or drinker who's trying to quit knows the feeling: You'll not only recall the rituals involved, but very specific images. Those in recovery often get confused by

the onset, as if their addiction has gotten worse somehow. No one ever told them to expect this part. . . . . It will be the most intense moments of your recovery, demanding your entire physical exertion and a Herculean effort to choose something else. You'll be exhausted. This will bother some, but withdrawal from porn can be filled with as much agitation, depression, and sleeplessness as detoxing from alcohol, cocaine, and other hard drugs.[273]

Knowing that withdrawal is a reality of overcoming porn addiction (and being prepared for it) is vital. Embracing difficulty, pain, and struggle are not natural tendencies, but that is the price of true freedom. Understanding that the journey will be difficult is important; planning for how to deal with that difficulty is even more important.

Park's experience mirrors that of many former porn addicts I have spoken with. That's why it's important to acknowledge the challenge and learn how to handle the inevitable failures and relapses. The way we handle failure determines our ultimate success.

Simply put, facing withdrawal is a struggle. Most people stumble at some point. But how do we handle those stumbles? Will we build an even stronger resolve to free ourselves from porn? Or will we suffer a major relapse?

The road to recovery is not straight and smooth. Beating any kind of addiction is a non-linear process. So give yourself some grace. You are fighting a difficult battle. *The key to winning that battle is to regroup, not relapse.*

Identify Your Triggers

"Know thyself" is critical wisdom for a journey to freedom from porn. It is essential to identify and understand what triggers your porn use so that you can prevent relapse. Dr. Elliot Berkman, psychology professor and associate managing director of the University of Oregon's Center for Translational Neuroscience, says that all habits have "cues" (sometimes called triggers).[274]

For example, if you are a smoker, the cue might be sitting down with a glass of wine or driving home from work. "You're most likely to relapse in the context of when you've done it before," Berkman adds. "Knowing your triggers can help you avoid them or better prepare to engage with them."[275]

So, ask yourself "What are my triggers?" Then list them and study your list. It could be when anxiety rises in you, when you feel angry, or when you feel stressed.

It could be when you feel sexual rejection or when your partner is unavailable sexually. Maybe you feel triggered when you see a couple being affectionate or when you see a sexually attractive person. Maybe it's when you feel lonely or insecure. Take time to discover and write down all the triggers specific to you.

In his book *Sex Addiction Cure: How To Overcome Porn Addiction and Sexual Compulsion*, former porn addict Matt Peplinski helps readers identify triggers. He recommends using one's imagination and referring to past experiences to form probing questions:

- What would you use to watch porn? Would you use your computer? Your smartphone?

- What time of day would it be?

- What would you be doing immediately before using porn?

- What emotions would you commonly experience before viewing pornography?

- Which circumstances would lead to your viewing porn?

- When you think about your future, how could difficult feelings or situations make you relapse on porn?

- In your daily routine, when are you most vulnerable to relapse?[276]

Once you have identified your triggers, strive to avoid them. Of course, it is nearly impossible to avoid all triggers. They are a part of life. That's why we should identify them, become familiar with them, anticipate them, plan for them, share them with a support group or accountability partner, and create contingency plans.

One way to prepare yourself is to rehearse your triggers and your response to them. Vividly imagine the experience of coming face to face with your triggers. What will you do to avoid or resist them? Science has shown that mental rehearsals, also known as visualizations, help train our brains and bodies for real-life action.[277] (Think of Olympic divers and gymnasts, who spend hours mentally reviewing and rehearsing their dives or routines.) Review your scenarios again and again, each time overcoming the trigger by whatever means necessary.

Another way to prepare for facing triggers is the "if-then" plan. In his research on the self-regulation of goal pursuit, psychology professor Peter Gollwitzer discovered that the most effective plans for behavioral change "are those that specify when, where, and how you want to act on your goals by using an 'if-then' format."[278]

He explains: "Take drinking too much in the company of your friends as an example. In the 'if' part of the plan, you identify the critical situation that usually triggers your bad habit. Perhaps the trigger is being offered a drink by your friends. In the 'then' part, you specify an action that can halt accepting the offer, such as responding to it by saying that you prefer a glass of water today. And then you link the 'if' and the 'then' parts together by making an 'if-then' plan: If on Friday evening my friends offer me a drink, then I will answer: 'I prefer to have a glass of water today.'"[279]

If you think that sounds too simple to work, Dr. Gollwitzer notes that laboratory experiments and "an endless line of studies"[280] published in peer-reviewed journals and "conducted with children, adults, and old to very old people around the world have shown that 'if-then' plans significantly increase the rate of goal attainment . . . even for people who have problems with self-regulation in general (e.g., children with ADHD, people who suffer from addictions, and frontal-lobe-disorder patients)."[281]

Cut Off Access

For a season, you might find it helpful to remove or shut down your access points to porn—another helpful tool in your box. Recovery from porn addiction, especially in the early stages or immediately following a relapse, might require "going to extremes." This might mean relinquishing your computer to a friend and using one at a library. It could mean getting a not-so-smart phone (without Wi-Fi or 5G) if your smartphone is an access point. You might need to cancel subscriptions to pay-TV networks or streaming sites if they lure you into watching sexual content.

And you should definitely install permanent porn-filtering software on your computer, tablet, and mobile devices and be sure to throw away any physical material related to porn (magazines, DVDs, etc.). Cancel all memberships to porn sites. In short, identify all of porn's access points into your life and remove them.

Digital Detoxing

"Digital detoxing" is an emerging trend in today's tech-saturated world. People are embarking on tech-free retreats, and some emergent companies focus on helping people peel themselves away from their screens and connect with the "real world." One such organization is called Digital Detox, whose motto is "disconnect to reconnect."

Disconnect to reconnect is also a great way to think about beating internet porn addiction. We let go of a harmful component of technology and engage more fully with the real world around us.

This means engaging with other human beings, with animals, with the earth—putting your hands to a project that doesn't involve a screen. It's finding a hobby that doesn't require Wi-Fi. Getting into nature is scientifically proven to be good for your mental and emotional health. Studies reveal that being in nature profoundly affects our brains, our bodies, and our behavior. Being in nature reduces anxiety and stress. It increases our attention span, boosts our creativity, and enhances our ability to connect with other people.

"People have been discussing their profound experiences in nature for the past several hundred years—from Thoreau to John Muir to many other writers," says researcher David Strayer, of the University of Utah. "Now we are seeing changes in the brain and changes in the body that suggest we are physically and mentally more healthy when we are interacting with nature."[282]

There are endless ways a person can experience the beauty and majesty of the natural world: Climb a mountain, fish on a crystal river, sail an ocean. Ski, bike, hike, walk, kayak, or run. If physical exertion isn't your thing, take photos of all that breathtaking scenery, capture it on canvas, or simply sit back and soak it in. Nature is not the only way to escape the digital world and interact with the real one. Visit a coffee shop, farmers market, museum, or music festival. Travel to someplace you've never been. (It might be a place only a few miles from your home.)

Or, consider learning something new: a martial art, a musical instrument, a craft, or a form of cooking. Buy or check out a good book and read it somewhere that feels good to you, whether it's your local park or your favorite chair on your porch or deck. The idea is to move away from a digital life and to build a social life: a real life, in the real, beautiful, physical world.

Learning to Navigate Challenges

Even with all of the preparation, planning, strategizing, and visualizing, a porn-free existence doesn't happen easily. At times, resisting porn will feel like trying to hold your footing during a tsunami. That is why it is important to have a clear, practical, and effective strategy to employ when you face challenges.

After talking with experts on the topic (and people who have overcome porn addiction), I have identified three simple approaches that will help you deal with porn and its triggers and other challenges.

Disrupt

When the urge to consume porn rushes in, disruption should be the first response. Disruption means interrupting the normal course of things. We disrupt porn temptation by putting away our smartphones, closing a browser window, or turning off the TV. Disruption is a physical act that closes the road to porn.

It's important to realize that disruption doesn't come naturally to us. In fact, it often goes against our impulses and habits.

Disruption requires a mindful and purposeful commitment. Sometimes, this commitment means swimming upstream against the current of our instincts and habits. For example, in 1981 a crazed man aimed a gun at President Ronald Reagan and fired six bullets. Everyone surrounding the president ducked, fell to the ground, or took cover. But not Secret Service Agent Tim McCarthy. He instantly threw himself into the line of fire. He took a bullet to the chest for the president, because that's what he had been trained to do. It's what he had practiced, mentally and physically.

After the incident, one interviewer observed, "It would seem that one's natural reaction would be to duck. And yet, you jumped in front of the president. Was that as a result of the training you go through?"

McCarthy replied, "It probably had little to do with bravery and an awful lot to do with the reaction based upon the training."[283]

With practice, with training, you can disrupt porn's presence in your life. And it doesn't require a dramatic act, like jumping in front of a bullet. Often, making one simple life change can remove an entrenched habit. For example, a team of psychologists (led by David Neal of the University of Southern California) studied subjects eating popcorn at a movie theater. The cinema setting was the contextual cue, and, when given a bucket of popcorn, the subjects ate, even when they were not hungry, and even if the popcorn was stale.

However, when the subjects were asked to use their non-dominant hand to eat, the habitual popcorn-gobbling ceased. This study concluded that disrupting the automatic consumption pattern brought the subjects' eating under "intentional control." The unconscious habitual behavior stopped when the subjects became aware of what they were doing.[284]

Displace

After you have disrupted the behavior, you can use your brain's neuroplasticity to "disorganize and reorganize" your mind. This process of "displacing" involves replacing the old with the new, the lie with the truth. Old patterns (including attitudes and beliefs) are taken apart so that new and better patterns can be established. As we have seen, porn addiction is an addiction to an illusion. It is based on a series of deceptions. That's why employing truth to combat the fantasy effectively displaces the "old with the new."

So, when you get the urge to use porn, remember that the actresses' smiles and moans of pleasure are commonly forced and coerced by a pornographer who is trying to sell you a fantasy. One pornographer told me point-blank: "People think porn is so glamorous and attractive, but they don't realize that what they see as attractive on screen is completely different in real life. I mean, it requires take after take to get it that way. . . . When people ask me, 'Are you attracted to porn?' I always respond, 'What's attractive about a girl curled up in the fetal position in the corner sucking her thumb because her mind is so blown by what she just did?'"[285]

No, porn actresses' smiles do not reflect their real-life experiences. Through personal interviews, I learned that many of these young women were pulled into porn during difficult times in their lives. They were vulnerable and short on options.

And let's realize that men in porn often achieve their erections only with the help of prescription drugs. Porn performer Eric Swiss (whom we met earlier in the book) told me bluntly: "I see guys doing Caverject, which is the injectable steroid that you use to get your dick hard, and the reason that kills me so bad is because they are struggling so hard to get something that just doesn't exist. . . . They are willing to forgo sexual activity for the rest of their lives, because once you shoot steroids into your dick, you ain't getting a natural boner for a long time to come. This is untested shit, you know, it's made for quadriplegics to use; it's not made for recreational sex. Five years down the road, ten years down the road, it's not working anymore . . . ."[286]

What's more, the sex in porn causes the actors and actresses frequent and often life-threatening sexually transmitted diseases. For example, a four-year, peer-reviewed study concluded, "STD and HIV outbreaks have been well-documented in the heterosexual segment of the adult film industry. Data . . . showed that 18 percent to 26 percent of performers were diagnosed with at least one infection of gonorrhea or chlamydia each year, 72 percent of those being among women. . . . Nearly 25 percent of all STD cases among women were reinfections within one year."[287]

It is important to cultivate a knowledge of truths like these to counteract all the lies.

When porn tempts us, we must destroy the illusion behind the temptation, behind the desire. We might recall facts about porn's damaging effects on our lives, or its connection to serious problems around the world.

Case in point: We know that porn cultivates a demand for commercial sex, and that demand is why sex trafficking flourishes around the globe. Recognizing that porn use is perpetuating the harm of vulnerable young women can dismantle the erotic fantasy.

For example, I have seen pornographic material handed out in red-light districts, in a direct attempt to fuel prostitution. Many of the flyers and other marketing materials that are distributed feature the women whose services are for sale.

Redirect

After displacing the old fantasies and replacing them with new truths, the next step is to redirect your energy into healthy and rewarding alternative actions. Go for a run on the beach or your favorite trail, swim some laps, visit the park and play with the dog, cook a meal, go to the gym, visit a good friend, get ice cream, do yoga. You get the idea.

Here's how porn-recovery expert Andrew Ferebee describes redirection: "Get away from your computer or smartphone and stand up and take three deep breaths. Come back to the present moment and regain control of the urge. With each breath, notice the urge slowly fading away and channel this sexual energy into something productive."[288]

Here's why redirection is so key: When we relapse or regress, our primitive modes of functioning take over. Impulse grabs the steering wheel; reality-based reasoning climbs into the back seat. It can feel as if our minds have reverted to a childhood state.

As research has shown, toddlers, children, and adolescents don't function at the same cognitive level as adults. Young brains are prone to being hijacked by impulses or intense emotions, which drive their behaviors. Spend just one day with a toddler if you need a crash course on a brain operating by impulse rather than reason. In the process, you will learn the value of redirecting attention—away from unhealthy behavior and toward something better. This simple strategy works well when the desire to consume porn hits.

Redirection technique helps us form new, positive habits. For example, some people use porn when they are feeling anxious. Anxiety is their trigger. But if they go for a walk or a bike ride, they train themselves to relieve their anxiety with a healthy action, something that provides fresh air, exercise, a change of setting, and the chance to encounter an old friend—or make a new one. The cue is the same, but the alternative is much, much better.

The suggestions I've shared in the past two chapters are by no means exhaustive. But give them a try. Take tangible steps on your journey to freedom. For your convenience, here's a quick recap of the steps:

- Admit there is a problem; move past denial.
- Frame your struggle in a healthy way.
- Work to unseat the power of shame.

- Cultivate self-compassion.

- Develop a resolve to resist.

- Believe you can do it. Nurture hope.

- Find support communities and accountability partners.

- Engage with a therapist trained in porn addiction.

- Adopt new values about porn by educating yourself.

- Identify your triggers and try to avoid them. But be prepared to encounter them.

- Engage in "digital detox."

- When the urge to consume hits: Disrupt → Displace → Redirect

13

SO, YOUR PARTNER IS CONSUMING PORN. . .

Perhaps you have endured the difficult experience of discovering that your partner is using porn. Like any form of intimate sexual betrayal, this is devastating. And it's not a male issue or a female issue; it's a human issue. Dr. Sheri Keffer, an author and family therapist, notes that "intimate deception crosses all boundaries, touching every age, socioeconomic line, gender, and faith."[289]

Regardless of the form it takes, an act of infidelity can be one of the most painful experiences of a person's life. For many, discovering a partner's porn use is a form of betrayal that can be as painful as an affair. Dr. Barb DePree, founder of the sexual health resource MiddleSexMD, notes, "Discovering that your partner uses porn addictively is a crushing, confusing experience. Women compare it to the betrayal of discovering an affair, except that the 'other woman' is a computer screen that is available 24/7 and that doesn't look or act like a normal woman."[290]

There's a reason we call it heartbreak. The pain of betrayal hits physically and emotionally. Research (led by neuroscientist and experimental psychologist Ethan Kross) reveals that experiencing infidelity activates the parts of our brains that trigger physical pain.[291]

Why is this form of betrayal so devastating?

Robert Weiss, a therapist and relationships expert (specializing in infidelity and addictions), explains, "For most people affected by serial sexual or romantic infidelity of a spouse, it's not so much the extramarital sex or affair itself that causes the deepest pain. What hurts committed partners the most is that their trust and belief in the person closest to them has been shattered."[292]

Dr. Berit Brogaard, author and professor of philosophy and the Director of the Brogaard Lab for Multisensory Research at the University of Miami, explains that the pain of infidelity is so deep because "it is one of the worst forms of betrayal of trust. . . . [I]t's because your rights have been taken away from you. . . . It is because you were deprived of something that you should have been taking part in (without the other person). . . . It's a violation of your right to enjoy those activities with your partner, a right others do not have."[293]

When two people begin a monogamous, intimate relationship, they build a foundation of trust in myriad ways. One person entrusts the other with their past, present, and future self. They entrust them with their body through acts of sexual intimacy. They entrust them with their emotions, and they offer their love.

Additionally, partners entrust one another with the physical aspects of their lives, such as finances, a home, and their most treasured belongings. Some of us also trust our partners with the sacred responsibility of parenting. In short, we trust our romantic partners on a variety of critical levels, and this requires a unique level of vulnerability. As best-selling author Terry Goodkind notes, "Only those you trust can betray you."[294]

Jennifer and David's Story

David was exposed to porn by a neighborhood friend at age 11. After that, he endured an on-again, off-again relationship with porn consumption. At times, porn nearly dominated his life. He could not overcome its temptations.

He was relieved when he met Jennifer. His craving for porn took a back seat to the intense excitement of the new relationship and his attraction to her. It was a whirlwind romance, and the couple soon married.

Shortly after their honeymoon, however, they reverted to old behaviors. Jennifer didn't tell David when they were dating, but she had struggled with depression for most of her life. When bouts of depression hit, she often lost all sexual desire. David felt deep hurt when his sexual longings were met with rejection. He had not revealed his long struggle with hardcore pornography either, and he soon returned to his cyclical porn consumption—doing his best to hide it from his wife.

> " Discovering that your partner uses porn addictively is a crushing, confusing experience. Women compare it to the betrayal of discovering an affair, except that the 'other woman' is a computer screen that is available 24/7 and that doesn't look or act like a normal woman."
>
> DR. BARB DePREE

Jennifer suspected something was awry when David began acting differently in bed. He no longer met her eyes when they made love. He felt distant from her, and he began asking her to do things she was uncomfortable with.

"Is there another woman?" she wondered. One night, she grabbed David's phone while he was sleeping. He wasn't texting a lover, as she feared, but what she discovered hurt her just as much.

His browser history revealed a seemingly unending list of porn links. Jennifer clicked on each one. The videos disgusted and appalled her. They made her feel jealous, rejected, and insecure. He stirred in bed, and she quickly returned his phone to its place on his nightstand. She curled up and quietly sobbed until she fell asleep, mentally and emotionally exhausted.

The next morning, David woke up early, as usual. He showered, got dressed, and headed for work. Jennifer avoided him, because she needed time to process what she had learned. (And she was unsure how she would react if their eyes met.)

She couldn't summon the will to go to work. She sat in her sweats all day, imagining various scenarios and wondering when she had lost her husband to these other women. Was it her fault that David was using porn?

How could I have let this happen? she asked herself. *Maybe it's my fault because I wasn't available enough when he wanted sex. Maybe I should have tried harder to lose weight or paid more attention to his needs. Maybe I am not exciting or attractive enough; it's no wonder he wants someone else.*

As the day wore on, Jennifer fluctuated between blaming herself and blaming David. Her emotions raged. She felt anger, betrayal, sympathy, disgust, fear, disappointment, and even hatred.

The storm of emotions made her feel like she was going mad. *Am I crazy?* she wondered. *Am I making a big deal out of nothing? Is this just what guys do these days, and I am the foolish one for not knowing that? Am I overreacting?*

However, Jennifer couldn't shake the sinking feeling that she had been betrayed by the person she loved most. When David returned from work, she asked him to join her in the bedroom. Sobbing violently, she revealed what she had discovered the night before, and how she felt about it.

His face went pale. Embarrassment and shame enveloped him, and he didn't know what to say or how to react. "I'm sorry," he said, staring at the floor.

Jennifer and David's story is not uncommon. And it should be noted that sometimes it's the husband who discovers his wife's porn use. The discoveries and disclosures play out differently, but this form of betrayal is traumatic for most couples.

Intimate Sexual Betrayal and Trauma

Dr. Barbara Steffens is an expert in sexual addiction and sexual betrayal. She has counseled the partners of sexual addicts for more than 20 years. In one of her books (written with Marsha Means), she notes, "When women and men talk about what they felt and experienced during their partners' disclosures (or the discoveries they made of spouses' secret lives), they often say they felt assaulted by the information they heard or saw. In their own words, hurt partners describe life-changing, world-shattering events in their lives. Events of such magnitude are normally considered traumatic."[295]

Indeed, the trauma of the discovery and disclosure of any form of sexual addiction is very real. The American Psychological Association defines trauma as "an emotional response to a terrible event."[296] An act of infidelity is a terrible event for most people. For decades, trauma and post-traumatic stress (caused by war, crime, natural disasters, serious illness, etc.) have been recognized for their impact on our lives.

However, clinicians and researchers are only beginning to understand "relational trauma." Relational traumas, sometimes called attachment injuries, occur when one person "betrays, abandons, or refuses to provide support for another with whom he or she has developed an attachment bond."[297]

In recent years, researchers have gained a deeper understanding of the intense pain people experience when they are betrayed by someone close to them, someone they trust.[298]

Dr. Sheri Keffer, whom we met earlier in this chapter, is a victim of sexual betrayal. She calls this trauma "Intimate Deception Betrayal Trauma (IDBT)."[299]

The 64-Color Box of Emotions

A traumatic event in a person's life (including the discovery of a partner's porn addiction) can cause a roller coaster of emotions and reactions. If you are experiencing this trauma, give yourself permission to experience and process your emotions. However, try to avoid clinging to any emotion too tightly, or reacting to it too quickly. Recognize that it's normal to experience a flood of conflicting and fluctuating emotions. Like Jennifer, you might feel sorrow, anxiety, shock, betrayal, denial, shame, disappointment, jealousy, neglect, resentment, attraction, abandonment, rejection, pity, loathing, compassion, hatred, and love—perhaps all at once.

Your mind might feel like a ping-pong ball, bouncing from blaming yourself to blaming your partner; from condemning yourself to condemning your partner. Take heart—you aren't losing your mind. You are processing a traumatic experience. Allow yourself to experience and move through those waves of emotions that build up and subside, but don't try to handle them alone.

These dramatic, fluctuating emotions can cause sleeplessness, depression, chronic fatigue, loss of appetite, overeating, hypervigilance, immune and endocrine problems, mood swings, nightmares, panic attacks, and many other symptoms.[300] Experiencing trauma is a serious event in a person's life, and, if not taken seriously, its consequences can be debilitating and long-lasting. The chaos of trauma can make us seek a quick fix, anything to calm the storm and stop the pain. However, the journey to deep and lasting healing can be long. It's tempting to look for shortcuts, but this temptation should be resisted.

Resisting Shortcuts to Healing

After Jennifer confronted David about his porn use, he apologized profusely. He declared passionately, "I will never do it again, because I can see how much it hurt you." He didn't want to destroy their marriage; he valued it more than almost anything in his life.

When David made his vow, he meant it. He didn't want to hurt his wife, and his lust for progressively extreme pornographic content disgusted him. He was overwhelmed by shame. Jennifer and David both wanted change. After the initial confrontation and the ensuing confession, repentance, and commitment to change, they felt a sense of relief. That relief proved to be short-lived.

Soon, David was watching porn again, and striving to do a better job of hiding it. Every time he succumbed to temptation, he felt shame—and more distant from Jennifer.

Jennifer was exasperated and devastated when she found porn on David's laptop. She felt betrayed and rejected by his broken promise. The few remnants of trust she had clung to quickly vanished.

Jennifer and David's story warns us to resist the temptation to minimize, rationalize, or shortcut the recovery process. Resist that urge. Confrontation, disclosure, repentance, and a commitment to change are not the change. They are only steps on a long road to recovery. Couples must allow one another the time, space, and support needed to experience true change and authentic healing.

Enduring the discomfort of an open wound is difficult. By nature, we want to avoid pain and uncertainty at all costs. We tend to suppress negative emotions. However, it's worth summoning the courage to forgo immediate and temporary comfort in favor of investing the time needed to deal with a complex and deep-rooted issue. The long road offers the best hope for authentic, meaningful, and lasting healing. This healing can take years. That is okay. Take the time you need.

14

HEALING FOR PARTNERS OF PORN CONSUMERS

*"Although the world is full of suffering, it is
full also of the overcoming of it."*

—HELEN KELLER[301]

n the previous chapter, we covered the painful experience of discovering a partner's secret life of porn consumption: the concept of intimate sexual betrayal trauma and its impact on a person's life. We highlighted the importance of not rushing the recovery process, of allowing enough time to ensure authentic and lasting healing.

The following pages will describe practical steps for healing—steps recommended by experts in the field of sexual addiction and betrayal. Some of this advice was gleaned from Dr. Barbara Steffens and her book *Your Sexually Addicted Spouse: How Partners Can Cope and Heal* (co-written by Marsha Means). If you are a partner of a porn consumer and want help, I highly recommend it.

This chapter isn't an exhaustive treatment of the subject, but I have tried to provide helpful ways to move forward on the path of healing. The path from trauma and hurt to healing and happiness is neither smooth nor straight, and it will be different for each of us.

The harsh reality is that the journey to healing is circuitous, filled with setbacks and wrong turns. But take heart; many people have found healing from intimate sexual betrayal. It's not easy, but it's possible.

Finding a Support System

On your path to healing, you will need support. Reflecting on the untimely death of his friend and Alice in Chains bandmate Layne Staley, Jerry Cantrell observed, "Part of the healing process is sharing with other people who care."[302] There is a great deal of truth to that statement, regardless of context.

Just as addicted people need time and support to heal, addiction experts agree that affected partners need community and wisdom to cope with intimate betrayal. This means that couples should allow one another the space and time needed to get help from a healing community—and, preferably, a trained therapist.

This is why programs like Al-Anon (a recovery and support program for those in intimate relationships with alcoholics) were created. Lois Wilson, the wife of Bill Wilson (one of the two founders of Alcoholics Anonymous), observed that as groups of men struggling with alcohol addiction met in the Wilson living room, their wives sat waiting outside. She began inviting them to gather in the kitchen for their own meetings, where they could share their feelings and experiences. After all, addictions harm more than the addicted; they affect anyone in an intimate relationship with them. Those kitchen meetings proved to be immensely helpful and healing, and Al-Anon was born.[303]

From Al-Anon's model, other programs for partners of addicts emerged, including COSA (Co-Sex Addicts Anonymous) and S-Anon, which focus on supporting partners or family members of sex addicts. These support communities have proven to be helpful, regardless of the addicted person's willingness to seek help.

These programs provide communication with and support for people enduring similar struggles. As with other forms of trauma, feelings of isolation, anxiety, depression, and loneliness can set in. That's why guidance from others who have been there can be invaluable in navigating dark and difficult emotional waters.

Your support network can also consist of friends and family or other trusted people in your life. These people can be a sounding board for you, and they can be empathic, judgment-free, and compassionate shoulders for you to lean on. Sharing your story and struggles with a trusted family member, friend, or support person can be therapeutic. There is healing power in someone's bearing witness to your pain and supporting you in your healing.

Establishing Boundaries

When a person is betrayed, he or she can experience an intense sense of powerlessness. This was not your choice. Your agency—your sense of control over your life—was taken from you, at least temporarily. Steffens and Means explain:

> Traumatization strips us of our personal power—
> of our abilities to protect ourselves and our children
> from the pain and disruption that sex addiction thrusts
> into our lives—the re-establishment (or perhaps the
> first-time cultivation) of this personal empowerment/
> self-empowerment quality proves vital for our healing.
> For many, this loss of control can be terrifying. When

you said your vows or entered into a monogamous relationship, you expected that your trust in your partner's fidelity would not be shattered—shaking the foundation on which you built your life. But here you are, and you need to regain a sense of safety, control, and stability in your life. Some call this process cultivating self-empowerment.[304]

Your sense of safety, dignity, and emotional health is critical in your healing journey. That's why establishing boundaries is an important first step in rediscovering your personal autonomy and empowerment. Ask yourself, "What do I need to feel safe?" Maybe you need your partner to unlock their phone and give you regular access to their browser history.

> Forgiveness frees us from the resentment and anger toward the person who has injured us. It releases us from the debilitating negative emotions that hinder our emotional and spiritual healing and growth.

Maybe you need computer access to be in common areas of your home. At minimum, you'll want your partner to install filtering software on all devices. Also, consider eliminating all sexually explicit mainstream media from your home. It's possible that seeing sexual scenes could trigger painful memories and feelings for both of you.

If your partner is serious about rebuilding trust and helping you heal, he or she should be open to establishing the necessary boundaries. Of course, it's your partner's responsibility to respect those boundaries. You need to decide what you will do if your partner chooses not to help ensure your emotional safety after you have suffered trauma.

You might also need to set boundaries around your sexual relationship. Being sexually intimate may not feel safe, in the wake of your partner's porn addiction. Set the guidelines you need to protect yourself until you feel more comfortable. Don't engage in any sexual activity that might serve as a trigger. For some couples, this might mean sleeping in separate bedrooms or living separately for a while.

I realize that this advice can feel like a double bind for the betrayed partner. On one hand, they resist being sexually vulnerable with someone who has hurt them by betraying their trust. On the other hand, the wounded partner might worry that being sexually unavailable will drive the offender back into porn.

These struggles are often rooted in this false belief: "My partner's porn addiction is my fault. Maybe it's something I did—or failed to do." That leads us to our next topic: self-blame.

Resisting Self-Blame

One of the greatest challenges you may face during your healing journey is the temptation to blame yourself for your partner's actions. This self-blame can take many forms, but it usually stems from a core belief: "I am not enough." Such thoughts drain us of power, as we tell ourselves lies, such as . . .

"I'm not attractive enough."
"I'm not exciting enough."
"I'm not good enough."
"I must deserve what happened to me."

If you've had thoughts like these, you are not alone.
Along with self-condemnation comes a sense of shame. You may

feel embarrassed and humiliated that you "let this happen," as Jennifer did in the previous chapter.

The shame can hinder your recovery, as you hide what happened from the people who could support you. That's why it's vital to move beyond self-blame to the foundational work and support necessary to recover from intimate sexual betrayal.

A word of warning here: Some therapists and support groups subscribe to treatment models that can reinforce feelings of self-blame. This is because many therapists and support groups automatically label those suffering from intimate sexual betrayal as co-dependents and co-addicts.[305]

Dr. Steffens notes that in her 20-plus years of working with partners of sexual addicts, she has found that such labeling is harmful, especially in the early stages of the healing journey. Her book recalls the experience of a client named Ashley: "I went to a COSA meeting, a 12-step recovery program for partners of sex addicts, to seek support and encouragement from other women going through circumstances similar to mine. The first thing we had to do was state our name and say to the whole group that we were co-addicts. I felt like I had been labeled as a 'sick' person who needed recovery, and they didn't even know anything about me! According to the group, I needed to figure out why I chose to pursue a relationship with a sex addict. But I'm just a wife whose world got flipped upside down when my husband disclosed his porn addiction and his attraction to other men. I felt scared, frustrated, confused and hurt by that meeting."[306]

Fortunately, many professionals shun a co-addiction framework as they work with partners of porn consumers. (And Ashley's experience at the COSA meeting is atypical.) Instead, they view the betrayal through a trauma-focused lens as they strive to understand the struggles faced by partners of porn consumers. I firmly believe that this perspective provides a compassionate, validating, and helpful lens for interpreting the experiences, behaviors, and emotions of partners of sexual addicts. And it avoids blaming the suffering partner. I highly recommend a professional who works from a trauma-focused perspective.

To find a qualified therapist near you, check out the Association of Partners of Sex Addicts Trauma Specialists (APSATS) at apsats.org. APSATS was founded by pioneers of the trauma-focused approach. Their treatment model acknowledges the issue of traumatic stress.

Of course, humans and their relationships, histories, and behaviors are complex. To be fair, I should note that, sometimes, the injured person might be complicit in his or her partner's harmful actions. If that is the case, it's beneficial to acknowledge and understand that responsibility so that it can be addressed.

There is a difference between self-blame and self-inquiry. Part of the healing process might include asking yourself hard questions about your role in the relationship. Sometimes that's what it takes to move forward in a healthy and helpful way. These questions might include:

"Did I set appropriate boundaries in the relationship and make them clear to my partner?"

"Did I create—or help to create—dynamics that need to be changed?"

"Are my past experiences affecting how I view my current reality?"

By asking important questions in a thoughtful way (with the support of a therapist), it is possible to engage in self-inquiry and self-assessment that is positive, helpful, and non-condemning. This process in no way legitimizes a partner's destructive or addictive behavior.

Rather, this type of inquiry is part of a well-rounded healing process, one that moves away from blame, shame, punishment, and self-hatred toward a deeper understanding of and compassion for the complicated nature of human intimacy.

Reclaiming Your Self-Esteem and Self-Worth

Experiencing intimate sexual betrayal can make almost anyone question his or her self-worth. (Self-worth is defined as "the sense of one's own value or worth as a person.")[307] You might feel unworthy of fidelity, or that something is wrong with you. Dr. Berit Brogaard explains that "infidelity makes you feel that you are not good enough. Your self-esteem plummets. . . . Your beloved found someone else that was better and more attractive than you in his or her eyes. . . . You feel like trash, unworthy of being loved, unworthy of being. That feeling may be the greatest contributor to your misery."[308]

Owning these negative thoughts about oneself can be debilitating. That's why it's important to rebuild or rediscover your self-esteem. With the help of a counselor or a trusted support person, you can process your negative thoughts and beliefs and regain your sense of self-worth and self-esteem by internalizing truthful, positive beliefs. You can overcome adversity and thrive again.

Therapeutic Forgiveness

Negative self-talk can hinder one's healing from intimate sexual betrayal. Anger, resentment, and judgment toward one's partner also hinder healing. Such bitterness damages us emotionally and physically. If we remain unforgiving about the wrongs done to us, we give the person who has wronged us a position of power in our lives.

Robert Enright, author, professor, and president of the International Forgiveness Institute, says that when we forgive "we are no longer controlled" by the offender. Enright's research has shown that when we forgive someone, we release ourselves from the emotional grip of the perpetrator of injustice. Forgiveness isn't about releasing a person from responsibility, blame, or clearing him or her of wrongdoing. It is about releasing yourself.[309]

Forgiveness is a difficult concept to digest for those who have endured intimate sexual betrayal. The word forgiveness can seem repulsive. But forgiveness produces emotional and physical benefits, and it's an important element of the healing journey.[310] We should remind ourselves that forgiving someone doesn't mean we accept or justify the wrong he or she has done. Forgiveness does not condone or minimize injustice. Instead, forgiveness frees us from the resentment and anger toward the person who has injured us. It releases us from the debilitating negative emotions that hinder our emotional and spiritual healing and growth.

Forgiveness isn't psychobabble or only for the religious—it is a well-researched concept that produces tangible, positive results for those who practice it. Researchers Suzanne Freedman and Robert Enright studied the effects of forgiveness therapy for women who were victims of sexual violation. Their research revealed that it took an average of 14 months for subjects to reach a place of moderate forgiveness.

While the process can be long, Freedman and Enright found that forgiveness therapy reduced women's levels of depression and anxiety, while increasing their hope for the future. When the study's "control group" began their own forgiveness therapy, the positive results were replicated.[311]

Writing on the benefits of forgiveness, Steffens and Means explain, "Forgiveness acknowledges great pain and offense, then releases resentment, bitterness, and revenge. Forgiveness recognizes that release allows us to move closer to our own healing . . . forgiveness can set us free when we are finally able to offer it. Forgiveness is a process as well as an event; it requires an act of will and often, much time."[312]

It's important to emphasize that forgiveness should never be forced, manipulated, or coerced. Dr. Harvey Schwartz has noted that "organic forgiveness" lies deep in the heart and soul of every human being. Organic forgiveness, unlike coerced forgiveness, arises naturally, sometimes when it is least expected.[313]

Many people have found that prayer and meditation help them forgive. Sometimes, a dream or conversation becomes the catalyst. Others reach a place of universal love, where they clear away feelings of anger or resentment and embrace all human beings—including those who have done them great harm.

And remember, forgiveness is not a single step. Forgiveness is an idea, a concept. It should be contemplated, explored, and, ultimately, exercised—but only when the heart is ready.

I encourage anyone suffering from intimate sexual betrayal to try the ideas in this chapter. I know that sexual betrayal affects relationships in different ways. Some couples reconcile and continue their relationships. Others realize they need to part ways, because they can't agree on a healthy resolution.

I can't presume the best way forward for you, because the dynamics of every relationship are different. However, if you seek healing and self-empowerment via a supportive community, you will find yourself in the best position to make wise decisions about the future of your relationship.

Dealing with a partner's porn addiction is painful. And for the addicted party, the path to freedom and healing is incredibly difficult. The consequences are painful for all involved, including a couple's children, friends, and other family members.

Many couples have emerged from their struggles with a passionate resolve for protecting others, especially future generations, from porn's detrimental effects. Healing for compulsive porn users and their partners is a great victory, and it should be celebrated. However, the greatest victory lies in finding ways to safeguard our children so that they never have to suffer the damage that porn can do.

15

SAFEGUARDING OUR CHILDREN:
Preventing Exposure

"An ounce of prevention is worth a pound of cure."
—BENJAMIN FRANKLIN[314]

n previous chapters, I have detailed how children in today's tech-saturated world are being exposed to porn, and I have explained the multifaceted harms of porn exposure, consumption, and addiction—for children and adults. Porn's harm is physical, psychological, emotional, relational, and societal. If you are a parent (or anyone who cares about children's well-being), you might be grasping for ways to protect the kids in your life from the harms of porn and porn culture. I have good news for you: There are practical steps you can take to safeguard your children, and I will share them in this chapter, and the next.

In our modern world, technology is ubiquitous, from computers to smartphones to "smart TVs" to tablets and beyond. Porn has many ways to trespass into our children's lives. That's why it's so important for parents to be deliberate and strategic as they prevent porn's intrusion.

The first step is to create a partnership with your children. In an age-appropriate way, explain to the kids in your life why they need protection from porn. Educate them about the harms of porn exposure, including its potential long-term consequences. Ask for their insights and ideas. This will help them understand what you are trying to accomplish and buy in to your efforts. The partnership model makes protection from porn a shared goal, rather than a set of top-down rules imposed by out-of-touch adults.

In a partnership, kids take ownership for their physical, mental, emotional, and spiritual health. They learn values and convictions that will guide them for life. Once that partnership is formed, you can focus on the following tangible ways to prevent porn exposure:

1. Cut Off Access to Porn in Your Home

In your home, you need barriers to protect your kids from porn exposure. All access points to porn need to be cut off. Call your internet service provider (ISP) and your cable or satellite company and tell them you want to restrict all pornographic content. Some ISPs are more limited than others, but most of them allow filtering by restricting internet content before it gets to your router. (Comcast, AT&T, TWC, Charter/Spectrum, Verizon, Cox, Frontier, and Optimum all provide content filtering). Most providers also allow you to filter content according to TV ratings (such as TV-PG, TV-14, and TV-MA).

If your ISP does not have an "opt out" feature, you can still block pornographic content in your home, via your router. This method is a bit more technical, but it's free. And there are many online tutorials to guide you through the process. If you simply aren't tech-savvy, you can purchase a router already equipped with parental controls. There are many "smart" Wi-Fi routers available for purchase online, and your local electronics store might also carry them.

Implementing these safeguards for your internet service will make your home a more positive place. However, be aware that most electronic devices can access the internet via 3G, 4G, and 5G networks—which bypass your ISP and your router. Thus, harmful content can still find its way into a kid's life. That's why you should install porn filtering programs and apps on each device your family uses.

Parents have the ability and the responsibility to create and maintain these layers of protection for their children. For a current list of the top porn-filtering routers, a tutorial on blocking porn at your router, and a list of software and apps that block porn, visit raisedonporn.com/resources.

> **In today's porn-saturated world, no child should have unfettered access to internet-connected devices.**

In a perfect world, parents wouldn't have to shoulder the entire burden of protecting kids. Internet providers, who are in the best position to block pornographic content from children, should be sharing the load.

For example, the United Kingdom pioneered protective strategies under the leadership of David Cameron, prime minister from 2010 to 2016. Britain was the first nation to enact an "opt in" model for internet service providers, meaning that ISPs automatically block access to online pornography unless customers specifically opt in to access such sites. Further, a consumer could not opt in unless he or she provided legitimate age verification. (Another aspect of Cameron's campaign involved some of the country's largest providers of public Wi-Fi eliminating pornographic content.)

This pioneering effort was significant because most ISPs set up their services with the pornography filters automatically turned off. Thus, customers had to contact their ISP if they wanted porn sites blocked.

Cameron hoped his campaign would stop childhood exposure to violent sexual images, which he said were "corroding childhood."[315] For the sake of transparency, I should note that these efforts had mixed results. First, access to sites providing sexual-health information were inadvertently blocked, as were some religious sites. And, of course, young people found a variety of ways to "beat the system."

However, that doesn't mean the effort should be abandoned. Governments and private companies should continue searching for the best ways to enact effective yet common-sense measures to protect children from the onslaught of porn. (In addition to the UK, Canada, France, Germany, and Australia are exploring various options.) We must advocate for legislative changes that protect our children. Contact your representatives and demand that ISPs implement opt-in and age verification policies as a first line of defense.

2. Build Boundaries and Structure for Time Online

The safeguards described above are helpful, but they shouldn't provide a false sense of safety. Any internet-connected device can represent a threat to our kids, so there must be structure when it comes to using these devices.

As a parent, I find it helpful to realize that each internet-connected device in our home carries the potential to seriously harm the lives of my kids, via the hardcore pornographic content they might access through social media, texts, and emails.

As a parent who understands devices' potential for harm, how do you want to introduce them to your kids? With great care, right?

These devices are a necessity in our tech-oriented world, but they also pose serious threats. That's why we need to create structure around their use.

As you work to create structure for your kids, be mindful and intentional about their screen time in general. Determine where and when devices can be used. Controlling "time and place" will help you optimize internet safety in your home. I recommend setting a rule that electronic devices be used only in common areas of the home, where the content can be viewed by everyone. Also, make sure your children ask permission before using a laptop, tablet, etc. This will provide full transparency and allow you to monitor the online activity.

In today's porn-saturated world, no child should have unfettered access to internet-connected devices.

I realize that, for safety reasons, your child might need to communicate with you when he or she is away from home. However, there are communication options that don't require online access. To get a list of devices and apps that can be used as communication substitutes to smartphones for your children, visit raisedonporn.com/resources.

3. Be Proactive About Protecting Your Children Beyond Your Home

Employing the above methods will help protect your children (and everyone in your home) from the harms of porn exposure.

Of course, every parent knows that risks abound beyond the home. That's why every parent or guardian needs an action plan to mitigate the risks. This is not about helicopter parenting. It's about partnering with your children to protect them when their screen access is beyond your direct control.

Think of all the places children spend time beyond their primary residence. They hang out at friends' houses. They attend school.

They spend time at another family member's home (a step-parent, older sibling, older cousin, etc.). They travel by bus or van for various activities, like sports, music, or drama.

For their children's protection while at school, every concerned parent should talk with local school leaders to learn which, if any, safeguards are in place there. Your school's principal, teachers, and coaches, for example, should understand and respect your commitment to protect your children from porn exposure. They should partner with you in this effort.

Additionally, you should communicate with the parents of your children's friends, as well as with any family members that your children spend time with. Make sure these people understand and respect your boundaries. (Don't assume they share your boundaries and values.) Making this effort will provide an extra layer of protection for your children when they are beyond your watchful eyes.

4. Help Your Children Recognize and Listen to Their Conscience

Conscience.

Gut feeling.

Inner voice.

Intuition.

Moral compass.

All of the above are names we ascribe to an important inner guide we all possess. When we learn to hear and trust our conscience (or whatever we call it), we avoid making bad decisions that harm us and others.

Children need encouragement and guidance to help them recognize and respond to that guiding voice inside them. One way they can begin to build confidence in their conscience is to experience positive outcomes when they follow it.

As author Alfie Kohn puts it, "Children learn to make good decisions by making decisions."[316] They realize how a decision helped them avoid trouble, and they learn how to avoid more trouble in the future. Giving children the opportunity to make decisions is one way to help them develop the ability to follow their conscience, use discernment, and grow in wisdom.

Most of us have a story of our "inner voice" saving us from harm. Share your stories with your children to help them recognize what following their conscience or moral compass looks like. Talking through a decision-making process with your children is another great way to show them the importance of following their conscience. Coach them on questions they can ask themselves before making a decision. Encourage them to be alert to physical cues that might serve as a warning or a reminder. If a knot forms in their stomach when they are asked to do something, or their heart starts beating faster, there's probably a good reason. Danger might be lurking around the corner.

When something doesn't "feel right" or they are being coerced into a situation, kids need to heed their intuition, or "flight cue."

Author Gavin de Becker defines intuition as "knowing . . . without knowing why," adding that training our children to "listen to their gut" can keep them safe from potential harm.[317]

5. Prepare Your Children to Respond to Peers

Parents who follow all of the steps above still worry that their kids' peers will find a way to introduce them to porn. It's a nightmare scenario, but it's very real. That's why you must prepare your children to respond to peers who put them in this compromising situation. In an age-appropriate way, discuss specific scenarios that could unfold.

This can be uncomfortable, but a child needs to recognize danger in order to avoid it.

Help your kids identify red flags, such as, "My parents aren't home; we can watch whatever we want on TV." Then talk through the best response, and practice it. Kids practice speeches and presentations for school. They rehearse for school plays and programs, and they practice for sports. Help them practice standing up to peer pressure.

Here's another red flag: "Come here; I want to show you something on my phone." Teach your children to ask about the content first, before agreeing to view it.

Another red-flag situation is a friend who uses his or her devices in a bedroom with the door closed and locked. In that case, teach your children to be proactive by either leaving the room or suggesting a relocation to a common area where there is adult supervision.

Ask your children to come up with red-flag scenarios, and brainstorm ways to respond.

Role-playing with your children is an effective way to prepare them. Kids need to practice what to do and say in risky situations. Take turns assuming various roles in your scenarios. Encourage your kids to be assertive by making eye contact and speaking firmly and decisively. Remind them to use "I" statements and clearly express themselves: ("I don't feel comfortable watching that video. I'd feel better if we did something else.")

Children and adolescents also need to understand that no means no. No doesn't mean, "Let's negotiate." No can be a complete sentence. Encourage and empower your kids to say no—and mean it. Books can help with these conversations. We recommend *Good Pictures Bad Pictures: Porn-Proofing Today's Young Kids* by Kristen A. Jenson (Glen Cove Press, 2018). You can learn more about this book and other helpful resources at raisedonporn.com/resources.

By implementing these measures, you greatly reduce the risk of a child's exposure to porn. Because you are reading this book, I know you are helping your child or children avoid porn exposure, especially during the most tender years. As a fellow parent, I commend you for being proactive as you prepare your children to be healthy and whole human beings.

However, an honest discussion about safeguarding children would not be complete without recognizing that no tactic or rule is foolproof. No matter how hard you try to protect your children from porn exposure and no matter how sophisticated your filters are—or how closely you watch them—you are not omnipotent nor omnipresent in their lives.

Even the best-protected kids are occasionally vulnerable to exposure, given our hypersexual media world. Dr. Gail Dines is among the experts who have acknowledged that no parent can provide 100-percent protection, because pornographic content permeates nearly every corner of the modern world.

According to Dines, requiring parents to prevent all exposure to porn culture "is like asking them to protect their kids from polluted air. The culture is now toxic and [porn] seeps into everybody's lives."[318]

So what do we do? We do everything we can to protect our kids from being exposed. And we strengthen them. We arm them by providing the relationships, environments, and tools necessary to resist harm if exposure occurs.

16

SAFEGUARDING OUR CHILDREN:
Preparing for Exposure

*"Hoping for the best, prepared for the worst,
and unsurprised by anything in between."*

—MAYA ANGELOU,[319]

I Know Why the Caged Bird Sings

During the past century, we have learned a lot about the psychological damage suffered by soldiers who go to war. Studies have shown that the rates of veteran PTSD and its effects (including suicide) are incredibly high. The military is now trying to be more proactive in preparing soldiers for what they will encounter and giving them the tools needed to understand and process traumatic experiences. These measures represent caring, compassionate, and necessary steps to protect our men and women, both now and in the future.

While we can't directly compare porn exposure to the trauma of war, we know that both affect one's physical and mental health.

In the porn-saturated world our children are living in, we know they will be exposed to dangerous, hypersexualized, and pornographic images. Thus, we need to arm them with the understanding and the tools they need to navigate the minefields ahead of them.

Porn exposure can harm a child in many ways, and this harm can be long-term. I have spoken with adults suffering from a lifetime of sex addiction, an addiction sparked by a single instance of childhood exposure to porn. They describe how things snowballed after that, as porn use invaded their lives and their consumption spiraled out of control.

Back in Chapter 5, we met Jonathan, a recovering porn addict, who was exposed to porn at age 12, via one of his friends.

> A shame-free zone is more than a place. It's a family culture. It's the way we relate to our kids. It's the ability to separate the negative things they might do from who they are as people.

Because of that preteen exposure and what it led to, Jonathan has spent a lifetime trying to recover and reclaim what was lost at that pivotal moment. Could things have gone differently for him if he had been equipped with the right preparation and protective tools? I believe so.

Because porn exposure is nearly inevitable today, we parents must give our children the best possible chance to avoid damage by strengthening and fortifying them against porn's harm. This strengthening comes from giving our children what public health experts and developmental psychologists call "protective factors."

As the name suggests, protective factors safeguard children when they are exposed to risk.[320] Implementing protective factors in our children's lives will make them less likely to be harmed by exposure to porn and its toxic messages. These protective elements take a variety of forms—including strong and positive family bonds, active parental involvement in kids' lives, diligent monitoring of their activities and peers, clear (and consistently enforced) family rules, and a strong framework of trust that results in open and shame-free communication.

It's also important to cultivate media literacy, establish a paradigm of what healthy sexuality looks like, help children develop sexual integrity, and adopt a worldview that dignifies sex and rejects objectification.

This is not an exhaustive list of protective elements, but it is a very good start. I encourage you to search for even more ways to protect your kids and enrich their lives. It all comes down to one key truth: The best way to protect your children is to be an aware, educated, attentive, and engaged parent.

A parent who activates protective elements builds something vital in a child: resilience. Resilience is the ability to stay healthy even when exposed to a potentially harmful substance or circumstance.[321] A resilient child can overcome the adversity of being exposed to porn and living in a porn-saturated culture. Experts at Harvard University's Center for the Developing Child explain that one way to understand the development of resilience is to visualize a balance scale or seesaw. Protective experiences and coping skills on one side counterbalance significant adversity on the other. Resilience is evident when a child's health and development tips toward positive outcomes—even when a heavy load of factors is stacked on the negative outcome side.[322]

Because each child is unique, approaches to building resilience via protective factors should be tailored to individual circumstances and specific risks. That said, there are some protective elements that should work for almost any child. Let's examine them.

1. Supportive Adults

According to child-development experts, children who develop resilience share an important common factor: the presence of at least one stable and committed relationship with a supportive parent, caregiver, or other adult.[323]

The power of that one strong adult relationship is the key ingredient in resilience, according to a report from the National Scientific Council on the Developing Child, a multidisciplinary collaboration directed by Harvard's Jack Shonkoff. These supportive relationships provide the "personalized responsiveness, scaffolding, and protection" that children need to overcome negative experiences. "They also build key capacities—such as the ability to plan, monitor, and regulate behavior—that enable children to respond adaptively to adversity and thrive."[324]

As a parent, I know that each of us yearns to play that stable, supportive, and committed adult role in our children's lives. We want to be that source of comfort and guidance. We want to be there to answer questions, discuss emotions, and help our kids process difficult or confusing experiences. But that role doesn't just happen. We must build a foundation of trust with our kids, and that takes time and intentionality.

2. A Foundation of Trust

Trust is the key foundational element of a healthy, positive, and supportive parent/child relationship. We can't help kids navigate the dangerous terrain of a porn-saturated world if they don't trust us. Trust enables open communication, and it helps establish the kind of home environment where a child has the confidence to approach Mom or Dad with even the biggest challenges. Trust helps your child overcome relational and communication barriers like shame, fear, and embarrassment.

Building trust with your child is a process—a process that requires a long-term investment of time, emotional energy, and physical energy. Trust is built through experiences; it grows through time and testing. Researcher Ken Rotenberg (of Keele University in the United Kingdom) found that children develop trust in response to specific interactions they have with others. It is not something they apply universally.[325]

The interactions that build trust happen when we spend time with our kids. Being present in a child's life is essential, and being present means more than living under the same roof. It requires significant and consistent time spent engaging with one another. Building this kind of relational equity is a key element of trust, and you build equity by spending quality time together.

And let's remember that trust can't be developed without truthfulness. Research has shown that, from an early age, children differentiate between people who are trustworthy (based on their truthfulness) and those who aren't.[326]

In an experiment by researchers Melissa Koenig, Paul Harris, and Fabrice Clement, toddlers interacted with two adults who presented conflicting names for objects the children were familiar with. Some of these names were accurate; others were not. The children could tell which adult was telling the truth and which one was not. Later, the toddlers sought out the truthful adults, because they identified them as trustworthy.

After years of research on the ways children develop trust, Koenig and her associates concluded, "Children gather evidence quickly. So much so that they can lose trust rapidly when they witness inconsistency."[327]

This is why it's important to tell your children the truth. For example, if you tell your child, "The next time you don't come home by your curfew, you'll be grounded for a week," you must follow through. Consistency in discipline and correction builds trust with your children, even if they aren't happy about it at the time.

Also, we parents must value the importance of keeping our promises. Keeping promises is another form of telling the truth. If you tell your child, "I promise to attend your next soccer game," make sure you show up. No excuses.

Over time, if you consistently tell the truth by honoring all promises, you will demonstrate your truthfulness, and, in turn, your trustworthiness.

3. Open Communication

Trust enables you to initiate open communication with your children. Open communication is important because it helps children engage with their parents about their life experiences, both positive and negative. It allows them to share their concerns and ask questions. Open communication goes hand in hand with trust, because without trust, children will hesitate to share their experiences with you. The more we communicate openly with our children, the more they will trust us.

Communicating openly and frequently (in age-appropriate ways) about sex, sexuality, and the dangers of porn and porn culture is essential.

Such open communication means that we parents must overcome our fears of discussing these sensitive topics with our children. We might have to deal with our own issues of embarrassment and shame. (Many of us grew up in family environments where talking about sex and sexuality was taboo.) We might still carry that "culture of silence" with us.

It's time to end the silence, because it's preventing too many parents from establishing open and shame-free communication with their children about sex and sexuality. This can't happen. The messages from porn culture are coming in loud and clear.

We parents can't let our embarrassment block us from speaking openly about sensitive topics. Let's be bold as we communicate about sex with our kids. If we don't educate them, the world of porn will.

And let's remember that communication should be two-way. We need to do more than talk to our kids. They need to feel comfortable talking with us. They should feel welcome to initiate a conversation, rather than wait for us. We should establish a wide-open line of communication with our kids. They should feel free to confide in us about even the most intimate issues. That's the only way they will successfully navigate the challenges of growing up in a pornified world.

An open line of communication requires a safe and shame-free environment. Our kids should know that they can confide in us, in a zone that is private and without judgment.

4. A Shame-Free Zone

Shame and the harm it creates is one of this book's major themes. We'll focus on the topic again in this chapter, because I want to highlight the necessity of establishing a shame-free environment in your home. Otherwise, open communication with kids is impossible. If a child fears parental shame, he or she is unlikely to share difficult life experiences or ask sensitive questions.

Shame is a major reason that children don't report sexual abuse. (And, as we have learned, kids experience porn exposure as a form of sexual abuse.)

If our kids are exposed to porn, they might feel too ashamed to talk about it. Fortunately, there are many ways that parents and other caregivers can remove shame and other barriers to communication.

The first step is ensuring that your home and your relationship with your kids are free of shame.

A shame-free zone is more than a place. It's a family culture. It's the way we relate to our kids. It's the ability to separate the negative things they might do from who they are as people. For example, your child might be struggling in school. You can correct him or her for not studying for tests and failing to complete homework assignments. But you shouldn't use labels like "stupid" or "lazy."

Likewise, if a child acts out and hits a sibling, he should be held accountable for that action. But he shouldn't be shamed as a person or labeled as a bully or a mean kid.

In a shame-free environment, a child experiences consistent love, regardless of behavior. Bad behavior is addressed, but it doesn't define the child. Actions are separated from identity. A shame-free household culture gives children the confidence that what they do (or what is done to them) doesn't change who they are. And it certainly doesn't change how much they are loved.

In a shame-free culture, children feel empowered to approach parents with the heavy burdens that life dumps on them: When they've done something they are ashamed of. When they have heard or seen something disturbing. When someone has harmed them in some way.

If your child has been exposed to porn (intentionally or unintentionally), a shame-free culture greatly increases the likelihood that he or she will reach out to you and discuss what has happened. When a kid knows, "This won't change my parents' love for me or make them think less of me," it can make all the difference. This level of transparency and safety enables you to be the supportive parent that your children need.

A shame-free environment also means that talking about sex and sexuality is normal. Sex is not treated as a taboo subject that is referred to only in code—or not discussed at all. Human sexuality is not regarded as shameful, dirty, or embarrassing. Instead, in age-appropriate ways, parents and caregivers assure kids that sexuality and their developing bodies are dignified, worthy of respect, and beautiful.

Communication about sex is open, and the discussions provide context and meaning. Parents instill in their kids a deep respect and value for sexuality. As a result, kids learn that sex is not something to be treated carelessly or frivolously.

5. Sex Education: Beyond "The Birds and the Bees"

In this chapter, we have detailed the importance of open communication about sexuality. However, it's important to note that this communication is about more than "the talk": the stereotypical discussion of the birds and the bees. Effective sex education is an ongoing conversation, not a one-time event.

Further, it's worth repeating that sex education in most schools is woefully inadequate, as we saw back in Chapter 5. And I have attended many, many church services without hearing a single message about sex.

In most homes, parents aren't talking with their kids about human sexuality either.

This collective silence regarding sexuality leaves children vulnerable to being shaped by porn culture's toxic messages, by porn's story. Let's remember that sex is a powerful force in a young person's life. It can't be pushed aside or ignored. As one young man confided to me:

> I hadn't had any class in sex education. I hadn't spoken to my folks about what sex was or how to engage in a healthy relationship. . . . This left me confused and perplexed. How do I find out about this sex thing? How do I learn more about it so when my friends and I get

together at school, at least I'll know something, and I can contribute to the conversation or sound like I know what I'm doing? That's when I was first introduced to looking online at pornography; that's when I first started exploring what pornography was, at a really young age, when I look back at it.[328]

Adolescents need to learn about sex because they are driven to it by their biology. Sexuality is a powerful force bubbling up inside of them. It's also coming at them from all directions, via a variety of media, as well as from their relationships with their friends. Yet it is something rarely discussed with adults, particularly parents.

As kids' bodies are changing and hormones are raging, this newly discovered aspect of their humanity is scary, arousing, mysterious, confusing, and all-consuming. They need help understanding and decoding this overwhelming and important part of their lives.

This is why we parents must provide support. Leaving that support role to anyone else is gambling with our children's sexuality.

Be assured, porn will swoop in to usurp your role as sex educator and guide. Children and adolescents are naturally curious about sex, and they need to seek out sources for information. If they can't approach a trusted adult for some open communication, they will go to peers or to the internet, where a search for "sex" will produce endless links to hardcore porn.

Parents, don't let porn, peers, or even the school system take over your child's sexual education. Take the reins, because you are capable—if you take the time to develop the knowledge and tools. To that end, I highly recommend engaging in Dr. Dines's "Culture Reframed Parent's Program: Building Resilience & Resistance to Hypersexualized Media & Porn." This free online curriculum was designed specifically for parents by experts in the field.

This program will provide you in-depth training and scripts to follow as you discuss sex with your children. It will help you build your children's resilience and resistance to porn culture, while promoting their healthy development. For more information, visit raisedonporn.com/resources or parents.culturereframed.org.

Effective sex education goes far beyond anatomy, sexually transmitted infections, and how babies are made. Holistic sex education provides children a foundational understanding about what it means to be a healthy sexual being, and how to maintain sexual integrity. It means approaching sexuality and the act of sex with dignity, respect, and reverence.

Our culture abounds with noise about human sexuality. Sex is often reduced to mere recreation. But sex is more than that. It holds great intrinsic value. It bonds two people: physically, emotionally, and spiritually. It can bring forth life; it's a sacred creative force. It should be treated with reverence. All of these truths should be part of your children's sexual education. They should also develop the ability to analyze, decode, and think critically about today's hyper-sexualized media culture so that they can resist its dangers and damage. This brings us to our final protective element: critical media literacy.

6. Critical Media Literacy

Most of us understand the importance of literacy in the traditional sense—the ability to read and write. However, in our high-tech world, we need to expand our perspective on literacy. Most of the messages our children receive today do not come in the form of written words on the pages of a book, magazine, or newspaper.

Instead, they come from GIFs, video clips, emojis, songs, sound bites, and so on—via their laptops, smartphones, and tablets. To mitigate the harmful effects of pornography and hypersexualized media, we must equip our kids and young adults with critical media literacy.

According to the Media Literacy Project, "Media literacy is the ability to access, analyze, [and] evaluate media."[329] Someone with this kind of literacy is able to process, understand, and decode the "language" (the sounds, images, and symbols) of high-tech media. Media literacy applies to films, advertisements, video games, songs, pop-culture symbolism, and the many forms of communication featured across social media. I like adding the word *critical* to the mix because it emphasizes not just understanding media but evaluating it and determining its worth.

A critical-media-literate young person can interpret, analyze, and deconstruct the images and messages he or she encounters. UCLA's Douglas Kellner and Jeff Share explain that critical media literacy. . .

> " . . . deepens the potential of education to critically analyze relationships between media and audiences, information and power. It involves cultivating skills in analyzing media codes and conventions, abilities to criticize stereotypes, dominant values, and ideologies, and competencies to interpret the multiple meanings and messages generated by media texts. Media literacy helps people to . . . evaluate media content, to critically dissect media forms, to investigate media effects and uses, to use media intelligently. . . ."[330]

In other words, the ability to distance yourself from a media message and analyze it critically helps the brain process it in a way that provides context and meaning. Consider the difference between attending a concert as a fan and getting caught up in the experience versus attending that concert to write a critical, published review.

In the same way, we want our children to be able to navigate the landscape of modern media—and the onslaught of hypersexualized and pornographic images that abound there. If we can help them become critical-media-literate, they will be able to experience media with clear-eyed objectivity and ask questions like this:

> "What is this video trying to tell me about who I am and who I should be?"

> "Are these song lyrics true-to-life?"

> "Do the people behind this website really care about me, or do they just want to make money?"

> "Is this social media post based on facts, or is it just someone's opinion?"

The ability to interpret *the message behind the media* is freeing and empowering. Children with this ability won't become media victims. They will interpret what they see and hear with a critical eye and a sense of context. This ability makes all the difference when a child confronts today's ubiquitous pornified media, because it allows him or her to mitigate the dangers.

Critical media literacy is something that today's youth can (and must) learn.

Think of all the protective factors discussed in this chapter as the smoke alarms, fire extinguishers, sprinkler systems, and emergency escape routes in a home or office. They help prevent a disaster but also provide solutions when disaster occurs. As parents, we must help our children develop sexual integrity so that they can navigate the difficult terrain of a destructive, confusing, and hypersexualized media culture.

The best way to help a kid develop sexual integrity is through parental modeling. That's why we adults must develop and model integrity (and critical media literacy) ourselves. We should value the sanctity of sex, dignifying the sexual aspects of our humanity. We should reject all sexual objectification in our lives, including in the media we consume.

Setting this example is an incredible way to love and protect our children. When we show our kids what it looks like to live a healthy sexuality, we provide a memorable and helpful example. Yes, our words about sexuality are important, but our actions are more important. Let's strive to be the person we want our children to be.

17

WRITING A NEW STORY

*"If you want to change the world,
you need to change your story."*
—MICHAEL MARGOLIS[331]

The porn industry, controlled by a handful of mega-corporations, has colonized the sexuality of people born into the internet age. The industry has achieved this by telling a potent story about who men and women are, how they should relate to one another, and how they should engage sexually.

This insidious story sinks its hooks into us, regardless of age, race, socioeconomic status, or gender. Like a Trojan horse, porn has infiltrated our world, via the internet, and has plundered our psyches, our bodies, our bedrooms, our families, and our culture. But there is a path to resistance, and, in the words of author Chris Hedges, "Resistance is the supreme act of faith."[332]

Social-change movements begin with a few courageous souls who summon their faith and bravely tell a new story—one that cuts against the grain of social norms and offers new insight and understanding.

We need to reclaim the powerful role of storyteller from the money-hungry media corporations if we want to reclaim our humanity. For our sake and the sake of our children, our communities, and our world, we must reclaim the narrative.

In the not-too-distant past, we've seen major shifts in our mass consciousness, and these changes give us hope as we strive to craft a better story.

For instance, as the scientific evidence about the harms of cigarette smoking mounted, America reached a tipping point. In the early 1960s, almost half of American adults smoked. Today, most people regard smoking as a dangerous health threat. Laws have been passed to protect people, especially the young, from the toxicity of smoking. However, before this shift in public awareness, smoking was seen as completely socially acceptable, harmless, and even "cool."

Today, smoking is generally frowned upon, and it's being pushed further and further out of public and private life. According to multiple studies, anti-smoking campaigns have saved more than 8 million lives in the US alone over the past 50 years.

The effort to change the story about smoking began with a report from the Surgeon General, published in 1964. This report dispelled many of the myths associated with smoking and concluded that smoking causes lung cancer, as well as other serious diseases. That report inspired many campaigns and programs that spread the story to audiences, across a spectrum of media.[333]

We should recognize porn as a similar threat to our health and communal well-being, particularly that of our children. It is time to shine a bright light on this problem.

To do this, we must rewrite the story about porn, so that our culture recognizes it for what it truly is. We must spread the news about the vast research-based evidence on porn and its dangers.

We must replace porn's cover narrative with the deeper truth about the vast, research-based evidence of porn's harms.

Abraham Lincoln once said, "Public sentiment is everything. With public sentiment, nothing can fail; without it nothing can succeed."[334] Lincoln understood the power of the collective social conscience to shift popular understanding of an issue. That's exactly what needs to happen with porn today.

A New Story About Porn

The porn industry wants us to believe that porn is innocuous, harmless fun—a form of entertainment rooted in free speech and personal choice. Porn also bills itself as a healthy form of couples' therapy or a way to spice things up in the bedroom. It helps prevent rape by enabling men to exercise their sexual aggression vicariously. It's a rite of passage for young boys and girls and a helpful source of sexual education.

False narratives like these highlight the importance of seeing through the facade the porn industry is presenting—and confronting the truth.

Porn is none of the things its creators and distributors claim. Journalist and activist Sarah Ditum notes, "Pornography is not an utterance. It is a video record of an act. That act is exploitative, deeply misogynistic, profoundly racist, routinely abusive and largely coerced."[335]

Porn is also part of a system of sexual exploitation—a worldwide, multi-billion-dollar industry that profits from the commodification, violation, degradation, and dehumanization of the female body. Going beyond the problematic nature of the industry itself, the mass proliferation and consumption of porn is a dangerous mass pandemic. It's a pressing public health crisis that is harming us collectively, starting when we are children.

I don't use the term "public health crisis" frivolously. I believe that only when we realize the health threats that porn causes (including threats to emotional health, relational health, societal health, and sexual health) can we combat it effectively (and that includes legislatively). Some government leaders are realizing this.

For example, based on a vast body of evidence, the state of Utah put a stake in the ground and declared pornography a "public health hazard leading to a broad spectrum of individual and public health impacts and societal harms." In 2016, Governor Gary Herbert signed a resolution called the "Concurrent Resolution on the Public Health Crisis."[336]

Since Utah adopted the resolution, sixteen other states have made similar declarations about porn as a threat to public health: Alabama, Arkansas, Arizona, Florida, Idaho, Kansas, Kentucky, Louisiana, Missouri, Montana, Oklahoma, Pennsylvania, South Dakota, Tennessee, Texas, and Virginia. These formal declarations are important steps, and we need other communities, states, and countries to take similar actions. (It's important to note that these resolutions do not *ban* pornography. Instead, they encourage education and awareness, including promoting science and research that reveal porn's negative effects.)

Public-policy changes like these can transform public opinion. Public opinion, in turn, can create even more policy reform. In the process, porn will be redefined, and identified for what it truly is: a toxic distortion of humanity and sexuality.

Telling a new story about porn is critical. And this story must address the lies porn has told about us. Porn has imprisoned men and women in tiny boxes, boxes that are limiting and dangerous. But we can break free.

One of the benefits of stories is that bad ones can be replaced by something better, much better. Consider how America's story has changed regarding the value of women and people of color.

We can write a new script about sexuality, masculinity, and femininity, and we can share it with our friends, co-workers, and children. We can preach it from pulpits and teach it from lecterns. And we can share it in our homes.

A New Story About Us

In addition to a new story about porn, we need a new story about who we are as men and women and what it means to live as sexual beings. As noted throughout this book, research has revealed that childhood and adolescent exposure to porn is at an all-time high. Pornography has emerged as a primary source of sexual (mis)information for boys and girls, and it is shaping masculine and feminine identity and sexual appetites.

Children are seduced into conforming to porn's destructive script. A generation is losing its true sense of self. They are shaped by a porn-saturated culture rather than becoming their authentic and unique selves. Their best selves.

In porn's story, men are entitled to women's bodies. Women's bodies are just another commodity, objects of male penetration and denigration. We are told, "This is who women are, and this is what they really want." Porn's script perpetuates a predatory masculinity and a hypersexualized and objectified femininity.

Porn has convinced men that their masculinity is commensurate with their ability to show no emotion, compassion, vulnerability, or concern for others. Porn portrays men as sociopathic narcissists who get pleasure from sexually subjugating, humiliating, and inflicting pain on women.

Boys who grow up on this toxic story become emotionally and spiritually deformed men.

Girls who grow up in the narrative of Porn Universe come to believe that their value and attractiveness are tied to their "hotness," sex appeal, and sexual availability. In porn's story, a strong, empowered woman is, at best, someone who knows how to leverage her sexuality.

Our story has been hijacked, and it's time to get it back. Boys and girls, men and women, mothers and fathers—we must passionately reject the messages porn is feeding us.

Porn is grooming girls to become complicit in their subjugation. They are told that they deserve all of the objectifying, aggressive, degrading, and dehumanizing sexual treatment. Someone who follows this narrative loses her sense of self-identity. That's why it's time for us to reclaim our own story, our true identity.

We must liberate ourselves from the confines of porn's toxic story and reclaim our human dignity. It's time to silence the messages of porn and amplify the true story of who we are as men and women and sexual beings.

Our world needs authentic men and women, not fabrications of the culture. Let's create a story that respects women and values them for the diverse range of gifts they bring to our world—not merely for their sexuality.

We need to tell the full story about who women are: They are complex, deep, intelligent, caring, nurturing, strong, sensitive, capable, dignified, powerful, intellectual, emotional, spiritual, creative, athletic, familial, political, compassionate, relational, and so much more.

Women deserve autonomy, influence, happiness, safety, respect, and peace. They are searching for deep meaning and purpose. They have unique histories, memories, and experiences. They long to make an impact on the world.

Women are not part of a sexual buffet, meant to appease men's gratuitous appetites. They are the crown of creation. They are multifaceted beings who constitute half of humanity. They bring forth and nurture human life. They deserve dignity, respect, and reverence.

They don't deserve to have their majestic, mysterious, and powerful bodies, minds, and souls desecrated, degraded, and destroyed through pornography.

Modern society claims to offer women a seat at every table, with full rights. That's one reason why porn's story about women has no place in our society.

If we want women to be valued, we can't create or consume stories that depict them as hypersexualized objects.

> There is no true power in the serial use of women as sexual conquests. We need young men to know that their strength and courage are meant to fight injustice, not perpetuate it.

Don't we want our daughters to know that their true beauty and human value should be expressed in myriad ways, far beyond the superficiality of physical appearance and sexuality? Let's create a story that tells each woman, "You are a gift to this world. You should be celebrated for who you truly are, not for who porn culture says you should be."

Men, too, are not what porn culture portrays: mindless, roving sexual beasts without conscience. Men are not innately abusive, sexually demeaning, and hostile toward women. They are not what Porn Man represents: an erect penis with the sole mission of "getting off" at a woman's expense.

We need a story that portrays the many beautiful dimensions of manhood, and the fact that men are a gift to this world. They are innovative, creative, strong, emotional, and passionate—with a capacity for profound gentleness. It's time to portray men using their physical strength for good purposes. Men who desire intimacy as well as adventure. Men who yearn to be loved, respected, and truly known. Men of complexity and beauty.

We need our sons to know that sensitivity, compassion, vulnerability, and gentleness are all part of what make a man powerful. There is no true power in the serial use of women as sexual conquests. We need young men to know that their strength and courage are meant to fight injustice, not perpetuate it.

These are the stories we need to tell. These liberating stories fly in the face of all that porn culture has taught us.

As we tell a new and better story, we embrace the better angels of our nature and usher in a new generation of men and women grounded in a healthy identity. An identity based on honor, dignity, respect, empathy, and mutuality.

Going further, liberation from the confines of porn's story will require us to reflect on and reclaim our humanity. We need to rediscover the truth that the highest and best expressions of that humanity are based on love and compassion.

Love reveres the gift of our common humanity. It's one person assuring another, "Your value comes from more than the physical body you possess." Love honors the whole person and desires good for them, even when that requires sacrifice. Love is not guided by consumptive compulsions but by respect and dignity. It is the highest way of being in the world—one in which we and those around us are better off. Love is the only place of true joy, freedom, and safety.

Love is the antithesis of objectification and dehumanization. Love is a vision. It is an ethic, a way of being in the world, and it is ultimately a choice—a choice to value the freedom, dignity, and well-being of others. Let's choose love. This will bring freedom and joy into our lives, and it will remove the toxic identities that a porn-saturated world has dumped on us.

In addition to choosing an identity of love, let's choose to be compassionate. Through compassion, we share in the vulnerability, powerlessness, and pain of others. Our solidarity forges a path toward hope and healing. The compassionate ones are beacons of light for a dark and hostile planet.

Compassion is more than something we do; it is someone we become. It enables us to truly see, truly feel, and truly act. When we are compassionate, we live in the highest essence of our nature. We are authentic and fully alive. The porn industry operates on the basis of object sexuality—people using and discarding others as mere sex objects. Compassion forces us to see people in their humanity and vulnerability, as multidimensional beings.

When we claim our identity as loving and compassionate people, we disrupt the forces of objectification and dehumanization that propel and underpin porn culture—and the messages of that culture release their grip on us. That is true freedom. We can say, "Who am I? I am a loving and compassionate being. That's enough."

Let's claim our identity as loving and compassionate people so that we can become the most authentic versions of who we were created to be.

A New Story About Sex

We need a new story about sex—one that bestows sexuality with the reverence it is worthy of. Sex has become our culture's major passion, but porn degrades sex and robs it of its inherent value. In porn, sex is transactional, animalistic, and selfish. It's a recreational act with no deep significance. It's devoid of mutuality and empathy. As author and college professor Robert Jensen has said, "Though love defies easy definition, it's easy to identify the sexual-exploitation industries' answer to 'what's love got to do with it?': Nothing."[337]

Lacking a loving disposition, porn sex embodies contempt. It's used as a weapon against women—a way to inflict pain, communicate disdain, and subjugate the victim.

Even with all of its obvious flaws, porn has its apologists. A porn critic often faces hostile backlash:

> "You must be against sex."

> "You're just a conservative prude, pushing your political agenda."

> "You want to control what everyone does."

> "You need to loosen up and stop trying to ruin everyone's sex life with your Victorian ideals."

Pro-porn advocates also like to use clever rhetoric, claiming to be "sex positive." This language insinuates that opponents of the porn industry are against sex or "sex negative." However, no industry should be exempt from scrutiny, for the sake of those who consume its products.

Indeed, entire movements are dedicated to questioning and critiquing the agriculture industry and the fast-food industry. If someone is against eating a head of lettuce soaked in harmful pesticides, are they "vegetable negative"? Of course not.

Noting that porn sex is harmful does not make its opponents "anti-sex." It makes us pro-sex, because we are advocating for an understanding and expression of sex that is truly positive—one that recognizes that sex is meaningful and has indescribable value.

We are asserting that sex is a powerful creative force that can bring forth life and forge together the soul, mind, and body of two individuals. We are affirming that sex has intrinsic value because it is the ultimate point of intersection, the pinnacle of human intimacy. Our desire to be known and to know others—our desire to be seen, cherished, celebrated, understood, nurtured, cared for, and committed to—it's all manifested in the act of sex.

We need a return to this essence of sexual connection: its loving care, vulnerability, and intimacy—not just the physical pleasure. Dr. John Chirban, a clinical instructor in psychology at Harvard Medical School, puts it eloquently:

> The goal of sex can be defined in one word: fulfillment. . . . True sexual fulfillment is when physical pleasure occurs within the context of an intimate and loving relationship. In this way, fulfilling sex transforms what could be a pleasurable and merely mechanical event into an expression of intimacy and love. Therefore, we distinguish that sex engages us in different ways: emotionally, relationally, socially, spiritually, and also physically. It is complete when it connects with our core values and character.[338]

Love expressed through sex joins people together, and we have a deep instinctual need to be connected to one another. Although no one can define all that love is, deep connection, care, trust, desire, and commitment are all vital components. The emotions and feelings produced by our human chemistry and physiology demonstrate how sexuality is designed to be paired with human intimacy. As behavioral neuroscience expert William Struthers and others have put it, humans are "wired for intimacy."[339]

Robert Jensen, whom we met earlier in this chapter, says it beautifully:

> Much of the talk about sexuality in contemporary culture is in terms of heat: Is the sex you are having hot? What if our discussions about sexual activity—our embodied connections to another person—were less about heat and more about light? What if instead of desperately seeking hot sex, we searched for a way to produce light when we touch? What if such touch were about finding a way to create light between people so that we could see ourselves and each other better? If the goal is knowing ourselves and each other like that, then what we need is not really heat but light to illuminate the path. How do we touch and talk to each other to shine that light?[340]

Let's reclaim that light in our relationships and the way we see each other. That light will expose the utter barrenness of the porn industry and illuminate the path to a more loving and humane way of life. It's indeed time to proclaim a new story about sex. We can no longer accept passivity as a virtue when it comes to the safety of our children, relationships, families, communities, and the dignity of us all. It is time for a countercultural revolution. The power to bring about change is in our hands. We can change the status quo, and it begins with changing ourselves.

EPILOGUE

As the youngest of four children, I grew up in a sheltered environment. But, somehow, I saw the movie *The Accused* when I was only eleven. That movie, which centered on a gang rape of a woman in a bar, left a huge mark on me, a mark I have carried for my entire life.

Years later, I learned about human trafficking, and that knowledge brought back the flood of pain and emotional trauma that I first experienced during *The Accused.*

What I discovered about human trafficking broke my heart. I could not escape the pain of realizing that girls were being broken physically, mentally, and emotionally and sold for sex against their will.

As I began to investigate the commercial sex industries (pornography, prostitution, and stripping), I learned that, while not all of the women involved had been trafficked, they were all exploited.

I realized that the commercial sex business is, essentially, institutionalized sexual violence against women. Some are subjected to unwanted groping while they dance in strip clubs. Others appear in porn videos where they are coerced into performing sexual acts they never agreed to. And then there are those who are exploited in prostitution, being routinely assaulted and even raped violently.

I wanted to do something to help. I read everything I could to educate myself. I prayed vigilantly for about nine months, and ultimately decided to put feet to my prayers. In 2007, a widow donated $10,000 to help me fight human trafficking. This donation was the catalyst for creating Exodus Cry, a nonprofit fighting global trafficking and commercial sexual exploitation.

There was little information about human trafficking at the time, and I realized the need to educate others about this tragedy.

So, in 2008, I began making a documentary film. I visited scores of red-light districts and saw how pornography was the marketing vehicle for human trafficking. It was an integral part of the problem.

Creating the documentary catapulted me into fighting sex trafficking. Over the course of four years, I visited 42 cities, in 19 countries, on four continents. During my efforts to investigate and combat human trafficking, I saw again and again how this industry overlapped with pornography. I began building a team to help me with my efforts, in filmmaking and beyond.

We released the documentary on human trafficking (titled *Nefarious: Merchant of Souls*) in 2011. The film struck a chord with audiences around the world, garnered a host of positive reviews, and won a variety of awards, including Best First-Time Documentary at the California Film Awards.

I then decided that it was time to focus on pornography and the public health crisis it was creating. I wanted to document its impact on consumers as well as the human rights violations suffered by the performers in front of the cameras.

I created three documentaries, titled *Raised on Porn* (a companion film to this book), *Entering Pornland*, and *Beyond Fantasy*, which involved interviewing scores of porn performers, directors, and distributors. (All three films detail the harmful effects of porn, but *Beyond Fantasy* focuses on the way many performers are exploited and abused on porn sets. It also examines the disturbing trends of violent porn and "barely legal" porn.)

I read all that I could on the subject. I talked to a variety of experts in the field, including neuropsychologists and relationship counselors. And, of course, I spoke with many consumers of porn. All told, I invested ten years into these projects.

My efforts brought me to several conclusions about pornography. First, the way it is created is a form of sex trafficking. That's not an overstatement. Sex trafficking is using force, fraud, or coercion for the purpose of a commercial sex act, and that's exactly what porn involves.

Pornographers are very clever about enticing performers to comply with their directives. Many of them explained to me how they are able to get what they want from their performers. The bottom line: Porn is created against a backdrop of coercion. There is no advocacy for performers, and there is no accountability for producers.

This is why porn needs its own massive accountability movement—a unified, widespread social movement in which survivors of the sex industry are empowered to share the truth about what they have suffered, creating a context for systemic change. Porn is especially dangerous because it is a form of trafficking itself, but it is also the fuel for trafficking. It sparks a desire for illicit sex and pours gas on that fire. Porn influences men to develop sexual appetites that most women will not comply with.

Third, childhood exposure to porn (much of it unwanted), is creating a generation of men who think it's normal to pay for sex. It's also creating a generation of women and girls who think it's normal to commodify their bodies. That, of course, feeds into even more commercial sex, and, thus, more sex trafficking.

This book is a natural extension of my documentary work. As we conducted research and interviews for the films, I realized the need for a more extensive look at the subject of pornography. I wanted to help people understand it, and heal from it. I began working on this book in 2012, so what you are reading right now is the product of 10 years of work.

Porn is a huge problem in our society, but we are already making progress. For example, our Traffickinghub campaign (now a global movement) focused on the human rights aspects of porn. During our research, we learned that many of the individuals featured in porn were underage or non-consenting. As part of our campaign, we held the website Pornhub (and their parent company MindGeek) accountable for failing to verify the age of, and to obtain consent from, those appearing in videos on its site. As a result, Pornhub deleted more than 10 million videos. That was about 80 percent of all the site's videos at the time.

Another campaign we have launched is Protect Children Not Porn (raisedonporn.com), which is advocating for all sites hosting porn to require ID-based age verification for all site visitors. Unfettered access to pornographic content is criminal. It should not be the default mode. Children shouldn't have to opt out to avoid porn. All porn providers, including hosts and distributors, should have walls in place to protect children from accessing their content.

Our #ENDTEENPORN campaign (beyondfantasy.com) addresses the range of injustices experienced by teen porn performers. Our documentary miniseries *Beyond Fantasy* addresses three key areas of exploitation teens are facing, including being made to perform in scenes depicting child sexual abuse, suffering physical and emotional trauma through the creation of violent rape porn, and regualrly being exposed to debilitating and life-threatening sexually transmitted infections. As the film conveys, there is simply no humane justification for these tragedies. The #ENDTEENPORN campaign calls for the minimum age of entry to be raised from 18 to 21 for all porn performers. We partnered with 21 porn industry survivors to publish an open letter, and accompanying petition, detailing how using teens in porn is predatory, abusive, and is destroying impressionable young lives.

I hope this book will motivate you to take action. You can begin by joining the Exodus Cry movement at exoduscry.com to add your voice and support to these critical campaigns. And believe me, we absolutely need your voice.

I and those I work with have been inspired by the great abolitionist William Wilberforce, who, for decades, battled slavery by changing mindsets—and changing laws. He was the most important figure in dismantling slavery across the British Empire. It's important to remember that when Wilberforce faced off with slavery, it was an accepted part of society. Many influential leaders defended (and promoted) it. But Wilberforce changed the way people thought about slavery. He framed the issue in terms of human rights and whether or not people wanted a truly just society. He helped educate and enlighten people, and that was the catalyst for major change.

In that spirit, I encourage you to keep educating yourself (and your children). If you are a parent or other adult caregiver, Chapters 15 and 16 of this book will help you protect and support your kids. If you and/or your significant other have been affected by porn, Chapters 11 through 14 should be of special interest to you. I encourage you to read or reread them.

Right now, our planet is the site of a battle between the forces of love and lust. Lust is the fuel that drives people to visit strip clubs, consume pornography, and pay to have sex with individuals in prostitution. To the degree we participate in these activities, we fuel and perpetuate the commercial sex industries. Participation at any level has consequences at every level. The commercial sex world operates on supply and demand. Without the demand, there would be no supply.

Keep in mind that the nature of porn, like lust itself, is exploitative. It considers only its need to be satisfied, never the damage suffered by the people on both sides of the camera. Make no mistake; there is no "lovemaking" in porn. It is people consuming other people for self-gratification and profit.

Speaking of people "being consumed," the current systems of socioeconomic, gender, and racial inequality plague every culture around the world, and they marginalize large segments of the population. These vulnerable populations are the ones most frequently preyed upon by pimps, sex traffickers, and pornographers for exploitation in the commercial sex industries. For example, Melissa Farley's research (see Chapter 7) revealed that 75 percent of people involved in prostitution have been homeless at some point in their lives. Further, 85 to 95 percent of those in prostitution want to escape it but see no other options for survival.[341]

To overcome this exploitation, we must reclaim a sexuality that is guided by love and compassion. This kind of sexuality will never lead a person into the commercial sex world. And it will never lead a consumer to buy a lap dance, to hire a woman in prostitution, or view porn sites.

Let's take a stand against the lie that sex is a meaningless recreational act. There is nothing "liberating and empowering" about commercial sex. That's another lie. In fact, any claim that the commercial sex industries are harmless is a lie. I see hope, as more and more people are exposing these lies and demanding change. They demand justice for those exploited by porn and its allies; they demand protection for our children. They are telling Big Porn and Big Tech, "Stop profiting off exploitation, or be shut down."

Let's take an especially strong stand for our children. As I have noted in this book, porn is the prominent form of sex education today. Porn is filling an information void. Parents aren't talking to their kids about the critical issues of gender and sexuality. Never once have I sat in a church service and heard a message about these topics. And the sexual education being provided by schools is woefully inadequate. I formed my ideas about sex and sexuality based on what I saw in media and porn. The same was true for my peers, and, a generation later, it's true for today's kids.

We need to claim our identity as loving and compassionate people so that we can become the most authentic versions of who we were created to be. We need to help our kids find their true path. I want my daughter to know that her beauty, value, and worth as a member of the human family can be expressed in a broad range of ways, not just through physical attractiveness or sexuality. I want her to know that she is a gift to this world. She should be celebrated for who she is; not who the culture says she should be.

I want my sons to know that sensitivity, compassion, vulnerability, and gentleness make a man powerful. I want them to know that the gifts they offer this world are rooted in love and compassion, not the serial use of women as sexual conquests. I want them to know that their strength and courage are for fighting injustice, not perpetuating it.

Pornography, like stripping, is just another form of prostitution. Women are offered up to be purchased and consumed by men. On a digital level, their bodies are sold for sexual consumption. This must end. As a society, we need to proclaim that we will not stand for the sexual exploitation of women. It is simply unethical and unjust. We do not want exploitation for our daughters. We do not want it for our sisters. We do not want it for our mothers. Why on earth would we want it for our society?

Join the fight against sexual exploitation at
raisedonporn.com, beyondfantasy.com, and exoduscry.com.

ACKNOWLEDGMENTS

Thank you to all of you who shared your personal stories with me concerning porn's impact on your lives. Your vulnerability and bravery are powerful. Thank you to Peter Gloege, Todd Hafer, Pat Judd and Rick and Melissa Killian at Killian Creative for lending your incredible skills to this project. I also want to thank Dr. Harvey Schwartz for being a consultant for the book and consistently sharing his ideas, deep insights, and knowledge.

I also recognize the leaders in the movement who have been shining a light on this issue for many years and have built the foundation upon which we all now stand: Andrea Dworkin, Anna Bridges, Barbara Steffens, Caroline Heldman, Catharine MacKinnon, Clay Olsen, Chyng Sun, Dan Allender, Dawn Hawkins, Diana E. H. Russell, Don McPherson, Donald Hilton, Donna Freitas, Donna Hughes, Ernie Allen, Gabriel Deem, Gail Dines, Gary Wilson, Jackson Katz, Julie Bindel, Lisa Thompson, Mary Ann Layden, Melinda Tankard Reist, Melissa Farley, Neil Malamuth, Noah Church, Pamela Paul, Patrick Trueman, Rachel Moran, Robert Jensen, Robert Weiss, Sut Jhally, Tony Porter, William Struthers, and many others.

ENDNOTES

1. Marie S. Carmichael, Valerie L. Warburton, Jean Dixen, and Julian Davidson, "Relationships among cardiovascular, muscular, and oxytocin responses during human sexual activity," Archives of Sexual Behavior 23, no. 1, (1994): 79, https://link.springer.com/article/10.1007/BF01541618.

2. Dianne S. Vadney, "The Two Become One: The Role of Oxytocin and Vasopressin," Physicians for Life, November 2, 2007, https://www.physiciansforlife.org/the-two-become-one-the-role-of-oxytocin-and-vasopression/.

3. Erica R. Glasper and Elizabeth Gould, "Sexual experience restores age-related decline in adult neurogenesis and hippocampal functions," Hippocampus 23, no. 4 (March 5, 2013).

4. Hayley Wright, Rebecca A. Jenks, and Nele Demeyere, "Frequent Sexual Activity Predicts Cognitive Abilities in Older Adults," The Journals of Gerontology: Series B, (June 21, 2017), 47-51, https://doi.org/10.1093/geronb/gbx065.

5. Benedetta Leuner, Erica R. Glasper, and Elizabeth Gould, "Sexual experience promotes adult neurogenesis in the hippocampus despite an initial elevation in stress hormones," PLOS ONE 5, no. 7 (July 14, 2010), https://doi.org/10.1371/journal.pone.0011597.

6. Meagan Tyler, "Can we eroticise equality? On the politics of sexual desire," ABC Religion & Ethics, April 10, 2018, https://www.abc.net.au/religion/can-we-eroticise-equality-on-the-politics-of-sexual-desire/10094822.

7. Jennifer Welsh, "Key to Better Sex Revealed in New Study," Live Science, June 8, 2011, https://www.livescience.com/14498-emerging-adults-empathy-sexual-health-satisfaction.html.

8. "a humane sensuality based in equality" is a term frequently used by author and women's rights activist Andrea Dworkin. The first published source for this quote appears to be the book Intercourse, published in 1987 by Secker & Warburg. The book has since been revised and republished by Free Press and Basic Books.

9. "Internet Users in the World by Region: June 30, 2017," Internet World Stats, https://www.internetworldstats.com/stats.htm.
   (Recent estimates by Statista place the global online access figure at 59.5 percent, and more than 90 percent in the United States.)

10. Doug Gross, "Google boss: Entire world will be online by 2020," CNN, April 15, 2013, https://www.cnn.com/2013/04/15/tech/web/eric-schmidt-internet/index.html.

11. "Balloon-Powered Internet for Everyone," Project Loon, accessed January 30, 2018, https://x.company/loon/.

12. Mark Zuckerberg Facebook post, March 26, 2015, https://www.facebook.com/photo.php?fbid=10101993038596471&set=a.529237706231.2034669.4.
   Editor's note: Facebook, the company that owns platforms including Instagram, WhatsApp, and (of course) Facebook, rebranded itself as Meta in late 2021.

13. Peter Diamandis, "The 'Rising Billion' New Consumers Will Arrive by 2020," Huffington Post, (blog posted on April 6, 2015 and updated on December 6, 2017), accessed January 30, 2018, https://www.huffingtonpost.com/peter-diamandis/rising-billion-consumers_b_7008160.html.
   Editor's note: For more information on the SpaceX/Google partnership, see https://www.theverge.com/2021/5/13/22433982/elon-musk-spacex-internet-connectivity-deal-google-cloud.

14. Michael Seto, quoted in Mary Aiken, The Cyber Effect, (New York: Random House, 2016), 16. http://downloads.bbc.co.uk/radio2/shows/radio2-arts-show/cybereffect.pdf.

15. Dr. Gail Dines, personal interview, 2013.

16. Elisabet Häggström-Nordin, Tanja Tydén, Ulf Hanson, and Margareta Larsson, "Experiences of and Attitudes Towards Pornography Among a Group of Swedish High School Students," European Journal of Contraception and Reproductive Healthcare 14, no. 4 (2009): 277–284.

17. Megan S.C. Lim, Paul A. Agius, Elise R. Carrotte, Alyce M. Vella, and Margaret E. Hellard, "Young Australians' use of pornography and associations with sexual risk behaviours," Australian and New Zealand Journal of Public Health 41, no. 4 (June 29, 2017), https://pubmed.ncbi.nlm.nih.gov/28664609/.

18. Häggström-Nordin et al., "Experiences of and Attitudes Towards Pornography Among a Group of Swedish High School Students."

19. Lim et al., "Young Australians' use of pornography and associations with sexual risk behaviours."

20. Ibid.

21. Gary Wilson, "The Great Porn Experiment," TEDxGlasgow, May 16, 2012, (video, 16:28), https://www.youtube.com/watch?v=wSF82AwSDiU.

22. Julie Ruvolo, "How Much of the Internet Is Actually for Porn," Forbes, August 7, 2012, https://www.forbes.com/sites/julieruvolo/2011/09/07/how-much-of-the-internet-is-actually-for-porn/?sh=253824a25d16. See also: Ogi Ogas and Sai Gaddam, A Billion Wicked Thoughts: What the World's Largest Experiment Reveals About Human Desire (New York: Dutton, 2011). (Ogas and Gaddam, who are featured in Ruvolo's article, analyzed approximately 52 million sexual searches between 2009 and 2010, performed by approximately 2 million people. Two-thirds of the searches were by individuals residing in the US, while the rest were by residents in India, Nigeria, Canada, and the UK.)

23. Åse Dragland, "Big Data—for Better or Worse," SINTEF, May 22, 2013, accessed January 2, 2017, https://www.sintef.no/en/latest-news/big-data-for-better-or-worse/.

24. "Just How Big Are the Biggest Porn Sites?" YouPorn, April 5, 2012.

25. Dave Parkman, "Pornhub Insights Releases Stats for 2020 'Tech Review', Xbiz.com, April 9, 2021, https://www.xbiz.com/news/258472/pornhub-insights-releases-stats-for-2020-tech-review.

26. "2019 Year in Review," Pornhub Insights, December 11, 2019, accessed January 15, 2020.

27. Ibid.

28. Ibid.

29. "2018 Year in Review," Pornhub Insights, December 11, 2018. See also, https://www.pcmag.com/news/pornhub-reveals-explicit-traffic-numbers.

30. "2017 Year in Review," Pornhub Insights, January 9, 2018.

31. Andrew Tarantola, "How Much Porn Does the Internet Hold?" Gizmodo, April 5, 2012, https://gizmodo.com/5899327/how-much-porn-does-the-internet-hold.

32. Wilson, "The Great Porn Experiment."

33. Monica Herrera, "John Mayer's Sexually, Racially Charged Playboy Interview Sparks Outrage," Billboard, February 10, 2010, https://www.billboard.com/music/music-news/john-mayers-sexually-racially-charged-playboy-interview-sparks-outrage-959433/.

34. "The Motion Picture Production Code," March 31, 1930, accessed January 30, 2018, https://www.asu.edu/courses/fms200s/total-readings/MotionPictureProductionCode.pdf.

35. Julia A. Erickson, "With Enough Cases, Why Do You Need Statistics?" Journal of Sex Research 35, no. 2 (1998): 132. For a review of some of Kinsey's unusual findings, see https://www.thenation.com/article/archive/kinsey-report/. Editor's note: In 2009, the Kinsey Institute reported that 23.2 percent of men had cheated on their current partner. The percentage for women was 19.2 percent.

36. As summarized in The Nation, March 25, 2009. See https://www.thenation.com/article/archive/kinsey-report/.

37. Steven Watts, Mr. Playboy: Hugh Hefner and the American Dream (Hoboken, NJ: John Wiley & Sons, 2008) 48; and Elizabeth Fraterrigo, Playboy and the Making of the Good Life in Modern America (Oxford, UK: Oxford University Press, 2009). Page number n/a.

38. Watts, Mr. Playboy, 48.

39. Dines, personal interview.

40. Ravi Somaiya, "Nudes Are Old News at Playboy," BBC (bbc.com), October 12, 2015.

41. The quote about Playboy's origins is from British journalist Christopher Turner. It has appeared, in various forms, in several biographies and articles about Hugh Hefner.

42. As revealed in Britt Ekland's autobiography True Britt and media interviews.

43. Theo Sapoutzis (CEO of AVN Media Network from 2009 to 2015), quoted in David Moye, "Porn Industry in Decline: Insiders Adapt to Piracy, Waning DVD Sales (NSFW)," Huffington Post, January 19, 2013, http://www.huffingtonpost.com/2013/01/19/porn-industry-in-decline_n_2460799.html. See also, https://www.similarweb.com/top-websites/united-states for recent figures on the popularity of porn sites.

44. See https://www.relevantmagazine.com/culture/report-3-porn-sites-are-now-more-popular-than-instagram-wikipedia-twitter-and-netflix/ and https://www.similarweb.com/top-websites/united-states.

45. Somaiya, "Nudes Are Old News at Playboy," *The New York Times*, October 12, 2015, https://www.nytimes.com/2015/10/13/business/media/nudes-are-old-news-at-playboy.html.

46. https://www.goodreads.com/author/quotes/24712.Erwin_Raphael_McManus.

47. A popular quote from Sut Jhally. See, for example, http://www.sutjhally.com/articles/advertisingcultura/.

48. For more of Joseph Goebbels's quotes on propaganda (and other topics), see https://en.wikiquote.org/wiki/Joseph_Goebbels.

49. Gerald M. Capers, "John C. Calhoun," *Encyclopedia Britannica*, accessed November 24, 2021, https://www.britannica.com/biography/John-C-Calhoun.

50. Thomas Dew's comments are from his "Pro-Slavery Argument," written in 1832. See: https://www.encyclopedia.com/history/dictionaries-thesauruses-pictures-and-press-releases/text-pro-slavery-argument-1832-thomas-dew.

51. Versions of *The Hireling and the Slave* (which is in the public domain) are available on Amazon and other sites. Some claim to be copies of the original publication, but this cannot be verified.

52. George R. R. Martin, *A Dance with Dragons: A Song of Ice and Fire: Book Five* (New York: Bantam, 2011): [page 495, mass market paperback edition.]

53. Melanie C. Green and Timothy C. Brock, "The Role of Transportation in the Persuasiveness of Public Narratives," *Journal of Personality and Social Psychology* 79, no. 5 (2000): 701-21. See also, Melanie C. Green, Jeffrey J. Strange and Timothy C. Brock, Mahwah, NJ: Lawrence Erlbaum (editor), *Narrative Impact: Social and Cognitive Foundations* (New York: Psychology Press, 2002), 315-41.

54. The 1983 Francis Ford Coppola film *The Outsiders* was based on the 1967 S.E. Hinton novel of the same title. The "stay gold" line was inspired by the Robert Frost poem "Nothing Gold Can Stay."

55. Melanie C. Green, Timothy C. Brock, and Geoff F. Kaufman, "Understanding Media Enjoyment: The Role of Transportation Into Narrative Worlds," *Communication Theory* 14, no. 4 (November 1, 2004): 311-327, https://academic.oup.com/ct/article-abstract/14/4/311/4110790?redirectedFrom=fulltext.

56. Jennifer Edson Escalas, "Imagine Yourself in the Product: Mental Simulation, Narrative Transportation, and Persuasion," *Journal of Advertising* 33, no. 2 (2004): 37-48. See also: Jennifer Edson Escalas, "Self-Referencing and Persuasion: Narrative Transportation Versus Analytical Elaboration," *Journal of Consumer Research* 33, no. 4 (2007): 421-29; Jennifer Edson Escalas, Marian Chapman Moore, and Julie Edell Britton, "Fishing for Feelings? Hooking Viewers Helps!" *Journal of Consumer Psychology* 14, no. 1-2 (2004): 105-14; Green, et al. "Understanding Media Enjoyment": 311-327; and Michael D. Slater and Donna Rouner, "Entertainment Education and Elaboration Likelihood: Understanding the Processing of Narrative Persuasion," *Communication Theory* 12, no. 2 (2002): 117-244.

57. Melanie C. Green, Sheryl Kass, Jana Carrey, Benjamin Herzig, Ryan Feeney, and John Sabini, "Transportation Across Media: Repeated Exposure to Print and Film," *Media Psychology* 11, no. 4 (2008): 512-39. Editor's note: For more on Plato's view of storytelling, see https://thestorytellers.com/plato-on-storytelling/.

58. Dines, personal interview.

59. For detailed information on brain scans of psychopaths, see www.huffpost.com/entry/psychopath-brain-hardwiring-concern-for-others_n_3149856.

60. Paul Little (aka "Max Hardcore"), personal interview, 2013.

61. *Skinny Teen Addee Kate-BDSM-Finding Her Submissive*, Ranked #4 in "Most Watched" category on January 10, 2020. Accessed, via Pornhub, on January 10, 2020.

62. Donny Pauling (former pornography producer), personal interview with Magic Lantern Pictures, 2013.

63. I. H. Frieze and B. S. Boneva (2001), "Power motivation and motivation to help others." As cited in Annette Y. Lee-Chai & John Bargh (editors.), *The Use and Abuse of Power: Multiple Perspectives on the Causes of Corruption* (Philadelphia: Psychology Press, 2002) pages 75-89. See also, Power: The Inner Experience by David C. McClelland, (North Stratford, NH: Irvington Publishers Inc., 1975).

64. Eric Swiss, personal interview, 2013.

65. https://mannerofspeaking.org/2015/01/05/quotes-for-public-speakers-no-194-mary-catherine-bateson/.

66. Mark Hay, "The Oral History of the Money Shot," Vice.com, December 11, 2016. https://www.vice.com/en/article/qkbwd5/an-oral-history-of-the-moneyshot.

67. Marjan Javanbakht, PhD, Pamina Gorbach, Dr. M. Claire Dillavou, Robert W. Rigg Jr MD, Sixto Pacheco, and Peter R. Kerndt MD, "Adult Film Performers Transmission Behaviors and STI Prevalence," UCLA School of Public Health, Department of Epidemiology, Los Angeles, CA; West Oaks Urgent Care Center, Canoga Park, CA http://www.aidshealth.org/wp-content/uploads/2013/06/Adult-film-poster-STD-Prevention-2014.pdf. Archived http://archive.li/rhjvC.

68. These comments are from Andrea Dworkin's speech "Pornography Happens to Women," delivered on March 6, 1993, at the conference "Speech, Equality, and Harm: Feminist Legal Perspectives on Pornography and Hate Propaganda," held at the University of Chicago Law School. For the full text of this speech, see https://philosophy.tamucc.edu/texts/dworkin-pornography-happens-to-women

69. Niki Fritz, Vinny Malic, Bryant Paul, and Yanyan Zhou, "A Descriptive Analysis of the Types, Targets, and Related Frequency of Aggression in Mainstream Pornography," *Archives of Sexual Behavior* 49, no. 4 (November 2020). See also, A. J. Bridges, R. Wosnitzer, E. Scharrer, C. Sun, and R. Liberman, "Aggression and Sexual Behavior in Best-Selling Pornography Videos: A Content Analysis Update," *Violence Against Women* 16, no. 10 (2010): 1065-1085. doi:10.1177/1077801210382866.

70. Eran Shor, "Age, Aggression, and Pleasure in Popular Online Pornographic Videos," *Violence Against Women* (2018):14, doi:10.1177/1077801218804101. See also, *Aggression in Pornography: Myths and Realities* by Eran Shor and Kimberly Seida, (Milton Park, UK: Routledge, 2021).

71. Tanya Burleson, personal interview, 2013.

72. "The Gangbang of Riley Reid," AVN, accessed January 27, 2018.

73. Little, personal interview.

74. "No Mercy Anal Compilation: Tight Teens Relentless Rough Fucking Painal," Pornhub, accessed January 10, 2020. For more information on the criminal charges against James Deen, see www.cnn.com/2015/12/01/entertainment/james-deen-rape-assault-allegations-feat/index.html..

75. Shor, "Age, Aggression, and Pleasure in Popular Online Pornographic Videos" and Bridges, et al. "Aggression and Sexual Behavior in Best-Selling Pornography Videos."

76. "Hogtied 24," AVN, accessed January 31, 2018.

77. Jackie Knight, "Little Asian Step-sis Gets Stuck and Fucked," Accessed via Pornhub, March 11, 2019.

78. Cameron Bay, personal interview, 2013.

79. E. Swiss and Max Hardcore, personal interviews and recorded conversation, 2013.

80. Tim A., personal interview, 2013.

81. Pornhub homepage, accessed May 26, 2018.

82. Xvideos homepage "most popular videos," accessed May 26, 2018.

83. See the American Psychological Association's study of first exposure to pornography, titled "Age of First Exposure to Pornography Shapes Men's Attitudes Toward Women," published on August 3, 2017.

84. A total of 2,344 parents and young people participated in this research, which was conducted by Revealing Reality for the British Board of Film Classification and published on September 26, 2019. See https://www.bbfc.co.uk/about-us/news/children-see-pornography-as-young-as-seven-new-report-finds.

85. Nina Hartley (pornographic model and pornography advocate), personal interview with Magic Lantern Pictures, 2013.

86. Bente Skau, quoted in Miranda A.H. Horvath, Llian Alys, Kristina Massey, Afroditi Pina, Mia Scally, and Joanna R. Adler, *"Basically . . . porn is everywhere": A Rapid Evidence Assessment on the Effects that Access and Exposure to Pornography Has on Children and Young People* (London: Office of the Children's Commissioner for England, 2013), 24.

87. A. Cowell and E. Smith, Streetwise pornography research for Streetwise Young People's Project, Newcastle upon Tyne, England, 2009. See also, P. Nitirat, "Thai adolescents' sexual behaviours and school-based sex education: Perspectives of stakeholders in Chanthaburi Province, Thailand," Unpublished dissertation submitted for PhD to the University of North Carolina at Chapel Hill (2007). See also, Linda Papadopoulos, quoted in Horvath et al., *"Basically . . . Porn Is Everywhere,"* 24.

88. Kelly Wallace, "Teens spend a 'mind-boggling' 9 hours a day using media, report says," CNN, November 3, 2015, https://www.cnn.com/2015/11/03/health/teens-tweens-media-screen-use-report/index.html.

89. "The Common Sense Census: Media Use by Teens and Tweens (2019)," https://www.commonsensemedia.org/sites/default/files/research/report/2019-census-8-to-18-full-report-updated.pdf.

90. Natalie Blanton, "Why sex education in the United States needs an update and how to do it," Scholars Strategy Network, October 10, 2019, https://scholars.org/contribution/why-sex-education-united-states-needs-update-and-how-do-it.

91. Tanja Tydan and Christina Rogala, "Sexual Behaviour Among Young Men in Sweden and the Impact of Pornography," *International Journal of STD & AIDS* 15, no. 9 (2004): 590-93.

92. Nicky Stanley, Christine Barter, Marsha Wood, Nadia Aghtaie, Cath Larkins, Alba Lanau, and Carolina Överlien, "Pornography, Sexual Coercion and Abuse and Sexting in Young People's Intimate Relationships: A European Study," *Journal of Interpersonal Violence*, March 6, 2016.

93. C. C. Joyal, A. Cossette, and V. Lapierre, "What Exactly Is an Unusual Sexual Fantasy?" *The Journal of Sexual Medicine* 12, no. 2 (2015): 328-340, doi:10.1111/jsm.12734.

94. "2017 Plastic Surgery Statistics Report," American Society of Plastic Surgeons, accessed January 21, 2019, https://www.plasticsurgery.org/documents/News/Statistics/2017/plastic-surgery-statistics-full-report-2017.pdf.

95. Dr. David Veale, as quoted in Rowenna Davis, "Labiaplasty surgery increase blamed on pornography," *The Guardian*, February 26, 2011, https://www.theguardian.com/lifeandstyle/2011/feb/27/labiaplasty-surgery-labia-vagina-pornography.

96. Kali Holloway, "The search for the perfect vagina: Why labiaplasty is suddenly booming," *Salon*, February 25, 2015, https://www.salon.com/2015/02/22/the_search_for_the_perfect_vagina_why_labiaplasty_is_suddenly_booming_partner/.

97. "Female genital mutilation," World Health Organization, February 3, 2020, http://www.who.int/news-room/fact-sheets/detail/female-genital-mutilation.

98. Mary Bowerman, "Increase in labiaplasty as women strive for 'normal' look," *USA Today*, March 3, 2017, https://www.usatoday.com/story/news/nation-now/2017/03/02/increase-labiaplasty-women-strive-normal-vaginas-what-does-normal-vagina-look-like-surgery/98629662/.

99. Bowerman, "Increase in labiaplasty."

100. Michael Flood, "Exposure to pornography among youth in Australia," *Journal of Sociology* 43, no. 1 (2007): 45-60; Sonia Livingstone and Magdalena Bober, *UK Children Go Online: Listening to young people's experiences* (London, UK: School of Economics and Political Science/EU Kids Online, 2003, 2004, 2005); Patrizia Romito and Lucia Beltramini, "Watching pornography: Gender differences, violence, and victimization. An exploratory study in Italy," *Violence Against Women* 17, no. 10 (2011): 1313-1326.

101. David Buckingham and Sarah Bragg, *Young people, media and personal relationships* (London: Advertising Standards Authority / British Board of Film Classification / British Broadcasting Corporation / Broadcasting Standards Commission / Independent Television Commission, 2003), 38.
     See also: Rachel O'Connell, Joanna Price, and Charlotte Barrow, *Emerging trends amongst Primary School Children's use of the Internet* (Preston, UK: Cyberspace Research Unit, University of Central Lancashire, 2004); and Robert E. Freeman-Longo, "Children, teens and sex on the internet," *Sexual Addiction & Compulsivity* 7, no. 1-2 (2000): 75-90. See also, Horvath et al. *"Basically . . . porn is everywhere,"* 25.

102. Sonia Livingstone, Leslie Haddon, Anke Görzig, and Kjartan Olafsson, "Comparing children's online opportunities and risks across Europe: Cross-national comparisons for EU Kids Online," as cited in Horvath et al., "Basically . . . porn Is everywhere," 25-26.

103. O'Connell et al., quoted in Horvath et al., *"Basically . . . Porn Is Everywhere,"* 27.

104. Buckingham and Bragg, *Young people, media and personal relationship*; Kenzie A. Cameron, Laura F. Salazar, Jay M. Bernhardt, Nan Burgess-Whitman, Gina M. Wingood, and Ralph J. DiClemente, "Adolescents' experience with sex on the web: Results from online focus groups," *Journal of Adolescence* 28, no. 4 (2005): 535-540; and Livingstone et al., *Risks and safety on the internet* (2011); Mulley, *Sexual health survey 2013 findings presentation* (2013); in Horvath et al., *"Basically . . . porn is everywhere."*

105. Livingstone and Bober, *UK Children Go Online*; Livingstone et al., *Risks and safety on the internet*; quoted in Horvath et al., "Basically . . . Porn Is Everywhere," 24-25.

106. O'Connell et al., *Emerging trends amongst primary school children's use of the internet*, (Preston: Cyberspace Research Unit, University of Central Lancashire, 2004); and Patricia M. Greenfield, "Inadvertent exposure to pornography on the Internet: Implications of peer-to-peer file-sharing networks for child development and families," *Applied Developmental Psychology* 25 (2004): 741-750, quoted in Horvath et al., "Basically . . . porn is everywhere," 25, 80.

107. "How Young People Use the Internet for Health Information," The Henry J. Kaiser Foundation, December 2001, https://www.kff.org/wp-content/uploads/2001/11/3202-genrx-report.pdf.

108. Jonathan Daugherty (former porn consumer), personal interview with Magic Lantern Pictures, 2013.

109. Lea Winerman, "The mind's mirror: A new type of neuron—called a mirror neuron—could help explain how we learn through mimicry and why we empathize with others," *American Psychological Association* 36, no. 9 (October 2005): 48.

110. Donald L. Hilton Jr., "As a Swallowed Bait: How Pornography Addicts and Changes the Brain," paper presented at the "Stand for the Family Symposium," Brigham Young University Law School, March 6, 2010, https://www.scribd.com/document/85912001/Donald-Hilton-Address-Pornography

111. William Struthers, personal interview, 2013.

112. Thomas Emerson, *The System of Freedom of Expression* (New York: Random House, 1970), 496. See also Catharine A. MacKinnon, *Only Words*, 146.

113. Lionel Shriver, https://libquotes.com/lionel-shriver/quote/lbg5f1j. (This quote is from the book *We Need to Talk About Kevin*.)

114. Dr. Jeffrey Satinover, quoted in Morgan Bennett, "The New Narcotic," *Public Discourse*, The Witherspoon Institute, October 9, 2013, http://www.thepublicdiscourse.com/2013/10/10846/.

115. "What Is Addiction?" American Psychiatric Association, accessed January 19, 2018, https://www.psychiatry.org/patients-families/addiction/what-is-addiction. Editor's note: The American Psychiatric Association and the American Psychological Association both use the abbreviation APA.

116. "Definition of Addiction," American Society of Addiction Medicine, accessed January 19, 2018, https://www.asam.org/resources/definition-of-addiction. See also, Howard J. Shaffer and Morris E. Chafetz, ed., *Overcoming Addiction: Find an effective path toward recovery*, A Harvard Medical School Special Health Report, (Cambridge, MA: Harvard Health Publishing, 2017).

117. David J. Linden, "The Neuroscience of Pleasure," *Huffington Post*, July 7, 2011, https://www.huffingtonpost.com/david-j-linden/compass-pleasure_b_890342.html.

118. Linden, "The Neuroscience of Pleasure." (Editor's note: According to Linden, the hippocampus is the foundation of memory in the brain and part of the reward circuit. It preserves agreeable memories that are associated with a pleasurable stimulus, and, by association, it also preserves all of the details of the environment in which this pleasurable stimulus was received. Later, similar environments can recall the pleasurable memories preserved by the hippocampus and trigger a strong desire for the "reward" or pleasure.)

119. Shaffer and Chafetz, *Overcoming Addiction*. (Editor's note: There is some debate over whether the "fire together wire together" phrase originated with Donald Hebb or one of his associates.)

120. Shaffer and Chafetz, *Overcoming Addiction*. (Harvard Medical School Special Report)

121. Hilton, "As a Swallowed Bait," 4-5.

122. Eric J. Nestler, Max B. Kelz, and J Chen, "DeltaFosB: A molecular mediator of long-term neural and behavioral plasticity" *Brain Research* 835, no. 1 (July 17, 1999): 10–17, https://www.semanticscholar.org/paper/𝛥FosB:-a-molecular-mediator-of-long-term-neural-and-Nestler-Kelz/421aa54ebefa3c2b69 2b2dec45fa9ea30b7d3323?tab=abstract.

123. Kyle K. Pitchers, Margaret E. Balfour, Michael N. Lehman, Neil R. Richtand, Lei Yu, Lique M. Coolen, "Neuro-plasticity in the mesolimbic system induced by natural reward and subsequent reward abstinence," *Biological Psychiatry* 67, no. 9 (May 1, 2010): 872–879, http://www.biologicalpsychiatryjournal.com/article/S0006-3223(09)01270-0/fulltext.

124. World Health Organization, International Statistical Classification of Diseases and Related Health Problems, 11th edition, C72: Compulsive sexual behavior disorder, retrieved January 21, 2019 from, https://www.ncbi.nlm.nih.gov/pmc/articles/PMC5775124/.

125. Deanna L. Wallace, Vincent Vialou, Loretta Rios, Tiffany L. Carle-Florence, Sumana Chakravarty, Arvind Kuma, Danielle L. Graham, Thomas A. Green, Anne Kirk, Sergio D. Iniguez, Linda I. Perrotti, Michael Barrot, Ralph J. DeLeone, Eric J. Nester, and Carlos A. Bolanos, "The influence of ΔFosB in the nucleus accumbens on natural reward-related behavior," Journal of Neuroscience 28, no. 41 (October 8, 2008): 10272–7, http://www.jneurosci.org/content/28/41/10272.

126. Boris Schiffer, Thomas Peschel, Thomas Paul, Elke Gizewski, Michael Forsting, Norbert Leygraf, Manfred Schedlowski, and Tillman H.C. Krueger, "Structural brain abnormalities in the frontostriatal system and cerebellum in pedophilia," Journal of Psychiatric Research 41, no. 9 (November 2007): 753-762, https://www.sciencedirect.com/science/article/abs/pii/S0022395606001166?via%3Dihub.

127. Michael H. Miner, Nancy Raymond, Bryon A. Mueller, Martin Lloyd, and Kelvin O. Lim, "Preliminary investigation of the impulsive and neuroanatomical characteristics of compulsive sexual behavior," Psychiatry Research 174, no. 2 (November 30, 2009):146–151, https://www.sciencedirect.com/science/article/abs/pii/S0925492709001085.

128. Valerie Voon, as quoted in "Pornography Addiction Leads to Same Brain Activity as Alcoholism or Drug Abuse, Study Shows," by Adam Withnall, Independent, September 22, 2013, https://www.independent.co.uk/life-style/health-and-families/health-news/pornography-addiction-leads-to-same-brain-activity-as-alcoholism-or-drug-abuse-study-shows-8832708.html.

129. Philip G. Zimbardo and Nikita D. Coulombe, Man Disconnected: How Technology Has Sabotaged What It Means to Be Male, (London: Rider Books, 2016).

130. "Brain Studies on Porn Users & Sex Addicts," Your Brain on Porn, accessed November 24, 2021, https://www.yourbrainonporn.com/relevant-research-and-articles-about-the-studies/brain-studies-on-porn-users-sex-addicts/#brain.

131. Norman Doidge, The Brain That Changes Itself (New York: Penguin Books, 2007), 108-109.

132. J. Michael Bostwick and Jeffrey A. Bucci, "Internet sex addiction treated with naltrexone," Mayo Clinic Proceedings 83, no. 2, (February 2008): 226–230, http://www.mayoclinicproceedings.org/article/S0025-6196(11)60846-X/fulltext.

133. Efforts are being made in several US states and foreign countries, such as the UK, Canada, Australia, France, and Germany to implement restraints, including age verification. See, for example, "More countries consider biometric age verification to access porn sites," by Ayang Macdonald, biometricupdate.com, June 7, 2021.

134. D. L. Hilton, "Pornography Addiction—A Supranormal Stimulus Considered in the Context of Neuroplasticity," Socioaffective Neuroscience & Psychology 3 (2013): 20767.

135. The comments from Dan Bilzerian and Joe Rogan are from episode 857 of the podcast The Joe Rogan Experience.

136. Adam and Shay D., personal interview, 2013.

137. Donna Freitas, personal interview with Magic Lantern Pictures, 2013.

138. Personal interview with unnamed college male, 2013.

139. Personal interview with "Shep," college spring break male, 2013.

140. Scott R. Braithwaite, Gwen Coulson, Krista Keddington, and Frank D. Fincham, "The Influence of Pornography on Sexual Scripts and Hooking Up Among Emerging Adults in College," Archives of Sexual Behavior 44, no. 1 (2014): 111-23, https://link.springer.com/article/10.1007%2Fs10508-014-0351-x.

141. Chip McCall (porn consumer), personal interview with Magic Lantern Pictures, 2013.

142. Chyng Sun, Ana Bridges, Jennifer A. Johnson, and Matthew B. Ezzell, "Erratum To: Pornography and the Male Sexual Script: An Analysis of Consumption and Sexual Relations," Archives of Sexual Behavior 45, no. 4 (May 2016): 995, https://link.springer.com/article/10.1007%2Fs10508-016-0744-0.

143. Pauling, personal interview.

144. Jeff Mullen, (porn producer), interview with Magic Lantern Pictures, 2013.

145. .Dines, personal interview.

146. Research by Melissa Farley, as cited in Leslie Bennets, "The Growing Demand for Prostitution," newsweek.com, July 18, 2011, https://www.newsweek.com/growing-demand-prostitution-68493.

147. *The National Intimate Partner and Sexual Violence Survey: 2010-2012 State Report*, Center for Disease Control and Prevention, April 2017, https://www.cdc.gov/violenceprevention/pdf/NISVS-StateReportBook.pdf.

148. David Cantor, Bonnie Fisher, Susan Chibnall, Reanne Townsend, Hyunshik Lee, Carol Bruce, and Gail Thomas, *Report on the AAU Campus Climate Survey on Sexual Assault and Sexual Misconduct* (Rockville, MD: Westat, 2015),13, 35.

149. World Health Organization, London School of Hygiene and Tropical Medicine, and South African Medical Research Council, *Global and regional estimates of violence against women: prevalence and health effects of intimate partner violence and non-partner sexual violence* (Geneva, Switzerland: World Health Organization, 2013), 2. For individual country information, see United Nations, "Violence against Women," Chapter 6 in *The World's Women 2015, Trends and Statistics* (New York: United Nations Department of Economic and Social Affairs, 2015).

150. United Nations Children's Fund (UNICEF), *Hidden in Plain Sight: A Statistical Analysis of Violence against Children* (New York: Division of Data, Research and Policy, September 2014), 167.

151. For more on the Steubenville rape case, see https://lepageassociates.com/steubenville-rape-case/.

152. Swiss, personal interview, 2013.

153. Lindsey Tanner, "About 1 in 16 US women say they were forced or coerced into losing their virginity," *Los Angeles Times*, September 16, 2019. See also, Ilsa L. Lottes and Martin S. Weinberg, "Sexual coercion among university students: A comparison of the United States and Sweden," *The Journal of Sex Research* 34, no. (1), (January 1997): 67-76.

154. Ronan Farrow, "From Aggressive Overtures to Sexual Assault: Harvey Weinstein's Accusers Tell Their Stories," *The New Yorker*, October 10, 2017: https://www.newyorker.com/news/news-desk/from-aggressive-overtures-to-sexual-assault-harvey-weinsteins-accusers-tell-their-stories.

155. "Ron Jeremy: US adult film star indicted on 34 sex crime charges" BBC, accessed November 24, 2021, https://www.bbc.com/news/world-us-canada-58346125. As this book went to press, Jeremy's case was on hold, pending a mental health evaluation. See "Adult film star Ron Jeremy's sex-crimes case on hold for mental health evaluation," by Maria Puente, usatoday.com, March 17, 2022.

156. Shay Douglas, personal interview, June 5, 2018.

157. John D. Foubert, Matthew W. Brosi, and R. Sean Bannon, "Pornography Viewing among Fraternity Men: Effects on Bystander Intervention, Rape Myth Acceptance and Behavioral Intent to Commit Sexual Assault," *Sexual Addiction & Compulsivity* 18, no. 4 (October 2011): 212-23, https://www.researchgate.net/publication/230683362_Pornography_Viewing_among_Fraternity_Men_Effects_on_Bystander_Intervention_Rape_Myth_Acceptance_and_Behavioral_Intent_to_Commit_Sexual_Assault.

158. Martha R. Burt, "Cultural myths and supports for rape," *Journal of Personality & Social Psychology* 38, no. 2 (1980): 217, https://pubmed.ncbi.nlm.nih.gov/7373511/.

159. Facebook comments on the Harvey Weinstein story.

160. Ibid.

161. Wayne A. Kerstetter and Barrik Van Winkle, "Who Decides? A Study of the Complainant's Decision to Prosecute in Rape Cases," *Criminal Justice and Behavior* 17, no. 3 (September 1990) 272-276.

162. Elizabeth M. Perse, "Uses of Erotica and Acceptance of Rape Myths," *Communication Research* 21, no. 4 (August 1, 1994): 488, 495, 508.

163. Dolf Zillmann and Jennings Bryant, "Pornography, Sexual Callousness, and the Trivialization of Rape," *Journal of Communications* 32 (1982): 10, 13, 16–17.

164. Mike Allen, Tara Emmers, Lisa Gebhardt, and Mary A. Giery, "Exposure to pornography and acceptance of rape myths," *Journal of Communication* 45, no. 1 (1995): 5–14.

165. Ibid.

166. Min-Sun Kim and John E. Hunter, "Attitude-behavior relations: A meta-analysis of attitudinal relevance and topic," *Journal of Communication* 43 (1993a): 101–142; and Min-Sun Kim and John E. Hunter, "Relationship among attitudes, behavioral intentions, and behavior: A meta-analysis of past research, Part 2," *Communication Research* 20 (1993b): 331–364.

167. Blair H. Sheppard, Jon Hartwick, and Paul R. Warshaw, "The theory of reasoned action: A meta-analysis of past research with recommendations for modifications and future research," *Journal of Consumer Research* 5 (1988): 325–343.

168. Jill C. Manning, "The impact of Internet pornography on marriage and the family: A review of the research," *Sexual Addiction & Compulsivity* 13, nos. 2-3 (2006): 131-165.

169. Neil M. Malamuth and James V. P. Check, "The Effects of Aggressive Pornography on Beliefs in Rape Myths: Individual Differences," *Journal of Research in Personality* 19 (1985): 299, 300, 303–04.

170. Neil M. Malamuth and James V.P. Check, "The Effects of Mass Media Exposure on Acceptance of Violence Against Women: A Field Experiment," *Journal of Research in Personality* 15, no. 4 (December 1981): 436-38, https://www.sciencedirect.com/science/article/pii/0092656681900404?via%3Dihub.

171. John Stagliano, as quoted in Robert Jensen, *Getting Off: Pornography and the End of Masculinity* (Cambridge, MA: South End Press, 2007), 99. (Editor's note: Stagliano, a former pornographic film performer, is founder and owner of Evil Angel, a pornographic film studio.)

172. Michael Milburn, Roxanne Mather, and Sheree Conrad, "The Effects of Viewing R-Rated Movie Scenes that Objectify Women on Perceptions of Date Rape," *Sex Roles* 43, nos. 9-10 (November 2000): 645-664.

173. D. Zillmann and J. Bryant, "Effects of massive exposure to pornography," as cited in Chapter 4 of *Pornography and Sexual Aggression*, edited by Neil M. Malamuth and Edward Donnerstein (San Diego: Academic Press, 1980 and 2014).

174. Shawn Corne, John Briere, and Lillian M. Esses, "Women's attitudes and fantasies about rape as a function of early exposure to pornography," *Journal of Interpersonal Violence* 7, no. 4 (1992): 454-461.

175. Hilary Hanson, "Boy Rapes 8-Year-Old Sister, Blames It On Watching Porn On Xbox," *The Huffington Post*. February 5, 2014. https://www.huffingtonpost.com/2014/02/05/boy-rapes-sister-watching-porn-xbox_n_4732615.html.

176. Natasha Bita, "Children Attacking Other Kids in Sex Crimes, Major Surge Since 2012," *The Daily Telegraph*, October 10, 2016. http://www.dailytelegraph.com.au/news/nsw/children-attacking-other-kids-in-sex-crimes-major-surge-since-2012/news-story/01d3d518199c1a563d1a18b7716b0502.

177. Paul J. Wright, Robert S. Tokunaga, and Ashley Kraus, "A Meta-Analysis of Pornography Consumption and Actual Acts of Sexual Aggression in General Population Studies," *Journal of Communication* 66, no. 1 (2015): 183-205, https://academic.oup.com/joc/article/66/1/183/4082427.

178. Wright et al., "A Meta-Analysis of Pornography Consumption and Actual Acts of Sexual Aggression in General Population Studies," 185-205.

179. Elizabeth Oddone-Paolucci, Mark Genius, and Claudio Violato, "A meta-analysis of the published research on the effects of pornography," *The Changing Family and Child Development* (January 2000): 48–59. See also, Manning, "The impact of Internet pornography on marriage and the family," 131-165.

180. E. Oddone-Paolucci et al., "A meta-analysis of the published research on the effects of pornography," including Manning, "The impact of Internet pornography on marriage and the family," 138.

181. Neil M. Malamuth, Tamara Addison, and Mary Koss, "Pornography and sexual aggression: Are there reliable effects and can we understand them?" *Annual Review of Sex Research* (2000).

182. Scott B. Boeringer, "Pornography and sexual aggression: Associations of violent and nonviolent depictions with rape and rape proclivity," *Deviant Behavior* 15 (1994): 289-304.

183. Edward Wieckowski, Peggy Hartsoe, Arthur Mayer, and Joianne Shortz, "Deviant sexual behavior in children and young adolescents: Frequency and patterns," *Sexual Abuse: A Journal of Research and Treatment* 10, no. 4 (1998): 293-304.

184. W. L. Marshall, "The use of sexually explicit stimuli by rapists, child molesters and non-offenders," *Journal of Sex Research* 25, no. 2 (1988): 267-288.

185. Gordon C. Nagayama Hall, Richard Hirschman, and Lori L. Oliver, "Ignoring a woman's dislike of sexual material: Sexually impositional behavior in the laboratory," *Journal of Sex Research* 31, no. 1 (1994): 3-10; Anthony Mulac, Laura Jansma, and Daniel Linz, "Men's behavior toward women after viewing sexually explicit films: Degradation makes a difference," *Communication Monographs* 69, no. 4 (2002): 311-329; and Laura L. Jansma, Daniel G. Linz, Anthony Mulac, and Dorothy J. Imrich, "Men's interactions with women after viewing sexually explicit films: Does degradation make a difference?" *Communications Monographs* 64, no. 1 (1997): 1-24.

186. Dolf Zillmann, "Effects of prolonged consumption of pornography," Chapter 5 in Dolf Zillmann and Jennings Bryant, editors., *Pornography: Research advances and policy considerations* (London, UK: Routledge, 1989), 127-158. See also, Dolf Zillmann and Jennings Bryant, "Pornography, sexual callousness, and the trivialization of rape," *Journal of Communication* 32 , no. 4 (1982): 10-21.

187. Donna Dunn, quoted in *In Harm's Way: The Pornography Civil Rights Hearings*, by Catharine A. MacKinnon, and Andrea Dworkin (editors), (Cambridge, MA: Harvard University Press, 1998), 153.

188. Associated Press, "Gymnastics Doctor Larry Nassar Sentenced to 60 Years for Child Porn Crimes," NBC News, December 7, 2017, https://www.nbcnews.com/news/us-news/gymnastics-doctor-larry-nassar-sentenced-60-years-child-porn-crimes-n827401.

189. Will Hobson, "Larry Nassar, Former USA Gymnastics Doctor, Sentenced to 40-175 Years for Sex Crimes," *The Washington Post*, January 24, 2018, https://www.washingtonpost.com/sports/olympics/larry-nassar-former-usa-gymnastics-doctor-due-to-be-sentenced-for-sex-crimes/2018/01/24/9acc22f8-0115-11e8-8acf-ad2991367d9d_story.html.

190. Michael L. Bourke and Andres E. Hernandez, "The Butner Study Redux: A Report of the Incidence of Hands-on Child Victimization by Child Pornography Offenders," *Journal of Family Violence*, 24 (2009):183–91. (Editor's note: "Hands-on" was defined as "any fondling of children's genitals or breasts over clothing, as well as skin-to-skin contact including hand-to-genital, genital-to-genital, and genital-to-anus.")

191. Subcommittee on Oversight and Investigations, Committee on Energy and Commerce, US House of Representatives, September 26, 2006.

192. Stephen J. Grocki and Lam D. Nguyen, "How Computer Forensics Can Dramatically Improve a Case," *Internet Pornography and Child Exploitation* 54, No. 7 (November 2006). https://www.justice.gov/sites/default/files/criminal-ceos/legacy/2012/03/19/USABulletinNov2006.pdf.

193. Bourke and Hernandez, "The Butner Study Redux."

194. Dominique A. Simons, Sandy K. Wurtele, and Robert L. Durham, "Developmental experiences of child sexual abusers and rapists," *Child Abuse & Neglect* 32, no. 5 (May 2008): 549-560, https://www.sciencedirect.com/science/article/pii/S0145213408000586?via%3Dihub.

195. David Ley, "Can Porn Be Ethical?" Goop.com, accessed October 11, 2021.

196. A. Bleakley, M. Hennessy, M. Fishbein, and A. Jordan, "Using the integrative model to explain how exposure to sexual media content influences adolescent sexual behavior," *Health Education & Behavior* (October 2011): 530-540.

197. Michael Cusick, personal interview with Magic Lantern Pictures, 2013. (Editor's note: The names of the couple featured in this chapter were changed for privacy reasons.)

198. M. S. Carmichael, V. L. Warburton, J. Dixen, and J. M. Davidson, "Relationships among cardiovascular, muscular, and oxytocin responses during human sexual activity," *Archives of Sexual Behavior* 23, no. 1 (February 1994): 59-79, https://www.ncbi.nlm.nih.gov/pubmed/8135652.

199. Larry J. Young and Zuoxin Wang, "The neurobiology of pair bonding," *Nature Neuroscience* 7 (2004): 1048-1054, http://www.nature.com/articles/nn1327.

200. Michael Kosfeld, Markus Heinrichs, Paul J. Zak, Urs Fischbacher, and Ernst Fehr, "Oxytocin Increases Trust in Humans," *Nature* 435 (June 2, 2005): 673-676, http://www.nature.com/articles/nature03701.

201. James T. Winslow, Nick Hastings, C. Sue Carter, Carroll R. Harbaugh, and Thomas R. Insel, "A role for central vasopressin in pair bonding in monogamous prairie voles," Nature 365 (October 7, 1993): 545-548, http://www.nature.com/articles/365545a0.

202. Z. Wang et al., "Voles and Vasopressin: A Review of Molecular, Cellular, and Behavioral Studies of Pair Bonding and Paternal Behaviors," *Progress in Brain Research* 119 (1998): 483-499.

203. Dianne S. Vadney, "The Two Become One: The Role of Oxytocin and Vasopressin," *Physicians for Life*, Nov 2, 2007, https://www.physiciansforlife.org/the-two-become-one-the-role-of-oxytocin-and-vasopression/.

204. Hilton, "As a Swallowed Bait.

205. Jennifer P. Schneider, "The new 'elephant in the living room': Effects of compulsive cybersex behaviors on the spouse," (1998), as cited in A. Cooper, "Sexuality and the Internet: Surfing into the new millennium," *CyberPsychology & Behavior* 1, no. 2 (1998): 169–186.

206. Jennifer P. Schneider, "Effects of Cybersex Problems on the Spouse and Family," in *Sex and the Internet: A Guidebook for Clinicians*, A. Cooper, editor, (New York: Brunner-Routledge, 2002): 169-186. See also, Schneider, "The new 'elephant in the living room.'

207. Dolf Zillmann, "Influence of Unrestrained Access to Erotica on Adolescents' and Young Adults' Dispositions Toward Sexuality," *Journal of Adolescent Health,* Volume 27, issue 2, supplement 1 (August 1, 2000): 42.

208. Schneider, "The new 'elephant in the living room,'" 178.

209. Raymond M. Bergner and Ana J. Bridges, "The Significance of Heavy Pornography Involvement for Romantic Partners: Research and Clinical Implications," *Journal of Sex & Marital Therapy* 28, no. 3 (May 2002): 193-206, doi:10.1080/009262302760328235.

210. Ana J. Bridges, Raymond M. Bergner, and Matthew Hesson-McInnis, "Romantic Partners' Use of Pornography: Its Significance for Women," *Journal of Sex & Marital Therapy* 29, no. 1 (January 2003): 1-14.

211. Annie Lobert (sex trafficking survivor), personal interview with Magic Lantern Pictures, 2013.

212. Schneider, "Effects of cybersex addiction on the family," 38.

213. Barbara A. Steffens and Robyn L. Rennie, "The Traumatic Nature of Disclosure for Wives of Sexual Addicts," *Sexual Addiction & Compulsivity* 13 (2006): 247–67.

214. Bridges et al., "Romantic Partners' Use of Pornography."

215. Bergner and Bridges, "The significance of heavy pornography involvement for romantic partners," 193–206.

216. Ibid.

217. Doidge, *The Brain That Changes Itself,* 104.

218. Anna Robinson, personal interview with Magic Lantern Pictures, 2013.

219. Jennifer P. Schneider, "Effects of cybersex addiction on the family: Results of a survey," *Sexual Addiction & Compulsivity* 7 (2000): 31-58.

220. Schneider, "Effects of Cybersex Problems on the Spouse and Family," (in Sex and the Internet: A Guidebook for Clinicians):169-186.

221. Monica Therese Whitty, "Pushing the Wrong Buttons: Men's and Women's Attitudes Toward Online and Offline Infidelity," *CyberPsychology & Behavior* 6 (2003): 569-79.

222. D. Zillmann, "Influence of Unrestrained Access to Erotica on Adolescents' and Young Adults' Dispositions Toward Sexuality," *Journal of Adolescent Health,* 42.

223. Ibid.

224. Dolf Zillmann and Jennings Bryant, "Pornography's Impact on Sexual Satisfaction," *Journal of Applied Social Psychology* 18 (1988): 448.

225. Ibid.

226. Jonathan Dedmon, "Is the Internet bad for your marriage? Online affairs, pornographic sites playing greater role in divorces," press release from The Dilenschneider Group, Inc. and the American Academy of Matrimonial Lawyers, November 14, 2002, https://www.prnewswire.com/news-releases/is-the-internet-bad-for-your-marriage-online-affairs-pornographic-sites-playing-greater-role-in-divorces-76826727.html.

227. Aristotle, *Politics,* 350 BCE.

228. Hyun Sik Kim, "Consequences of Parental Divorce for Child Development," *American Sociological Review* 76, no. 3 (June 2011): 498, http://www.asanet.org/sites/default/files/savvy/images/journals/docs/pdf/asr/Jun11ASRFeature.pdf.

229. Paul R. Amato and Bruce Keith, "Parental divorce and the well-being of children: A meta-analysis," *Psychological Bulletin* 110, no. 1 (July 1991): 26-46, https://www.semanticscholar.org/paper/Parental-divorce-and-the-well-being-of-children%3A-a-Amato-Keith/b04006969de7fdfea2aada728f734edd95e7571d.

230. Andreas Diekmann and Kurt Schmidheiny, "The Intergenerational Transmission of Divorce: A Fifteen-Country Study with the Fertility and Family Survey," ETH Zurich Sociology, Working Paper No. 4 (2004, 2008), http://repec.ethz.ch/ets/papers/diekmann_schmidheiny_transmission.pdf.

231. Jeff Mullen (porn producer), personal interview with Magic Lantern Pictures, 2013.

232. Stacey Nelkin, "5 Reasons Why Watching Porn Together Can Be Good For Your Relationship," *Huffington Post*, March 7, 2013, https://www.huffingtonpost.com/stacey-nelkin/5-reasons-why-watching-po_b_2766968.html.

233. Kendall Fisher, "Gwyneth Paltrow Wants to Improve Your Sex Life With 9 Goop-Approved Tips About Orgasms, Anal and More," *E! News*, March 23, 2017, http://www.eonline.com/news/838301/gwyneth-paltrow-wants-to-improve-your-sex-life-with-9-goop-approved-tips-about-orgasms-anal-and-more.

234. "Men aged 18 to 30 are taking Viagra to keep up with Sex and the City generation," *Evening Standard*, June 14, 2008. https://www.standard.co.uk/news/men-aged-18-to-30-are-taking-viagra-to-keep-up-with-sex-and-the-city-generation-6805116.html.

235. "Are Porn Tube Sites Causing Erectile Dysfunction?" Your Brain on Porn, January 16, 2013, http://www.yourbrainonporn.com/are-porn-tube-sites-causing-erectile-dysfunction; and "Porn-Induced Sexual Dysfunction Is A Growing Problem," Your Brain on Porn, July 11, 2011, https://www.yourbrainonporn.com/ybop-articles-on-porn-addiction-porn-induced-problems/effects-of-porn-on-the-user/porn-induced-sexual-dysfunction-is-a-growing-problem-2011/.

236. Online forum, NoFap, accessed June 22, 2018, https://www.nofap.com/forum/index.php?threads/new-to-this-whole-thing-struggling-with-ed-nofap-may-be-my-last-hope-need-reassurance.163184/.

237. Online forum, NoFap, accessed June 22, 2018, https://www.nofap.com/forum/index.php?threads/will-i-ever-be-able-to-enjoy-sex.178316/.

238. Online forum, NoFap, accessed June 22, 2018, https://www.nofap.com/forum/index.php?threads/pied.145709/.

239. "A Semantic Analysis of an Erectile Dysfunction Forum," Superdrug Online Doctor, accessed January 27, 2018, https://onlinedoctor.superdrug.com/semantic-analysis-erectile-dysfunction/.

240. Charlene L. Muehlenhard and Sheena K. Shippee, "Men's and women's reports of pretending orgasm," *The Journal of Sex Research* 47, no. 6 (November 2010): 552-67, http://www.tandfonline.com/doi/abs/10.1080/00224490903171794.

241. Jo Macfarlane, "Men Aged 18 to 30 on Viagra to Keep Up with Sex and the City Generation," *Daily Mail*, June 14, 2008, accessed: January 27, 2018, http://www.dailymail.co.uk/health/article-1026523/Men-aged-18-30-Viagra-Sex-And-The-City-generation.html#ixzz2yQcAJEbx.

242. Pauling, personal interview.

243. Doidge, *The Brain That Changes Itself.*

244. AK Jstar (pseudonym), "Newly Married Life Ruined Due to PIED," NoFAP, October 7, 2017, https://www.nofap.com/forum/index.php?threads/newly-married-life-ruined-due-to-pied.134070/.

245. Carlo Foresta et al., "Italian Men Suffer Sexual Anorexia After Internet Porn Use," ANSA, March 4, 2017, http://www.ansa.it/web/notizie/rubriche/english/2011/02/24/visualizza_new.html_1583160579.html.

246. Gary Wilson, "Start Here: Porn-induced Sexual Dysfunction," Your Brain on Porn, June 17, 2011, https://www.yourbrainonporn.com/porn-induced-sexual-dysfunctions/start-here-porn-induced-sexual-dysfunction/.

247. Justin Corley, personal interview with Magic Lantern Pictures, 2013.

248. Syed (pseudonym), "PIED Recovery Success Stories?" NoFap, September 4, 2017, https://www.nofap.com/forum/index.php?threads/pied-recovery-success-stories.126362/.

249. Gary Wilson, "Rebooting Accounts: Page 1," Your Brain on Porn, December 5, 2010, https://www.yourbrainonporn.com/rebooting-accounts.

250. Ibid.

251. Ibid.

252. Jayson Gaddis, host, "Porn vs. Having Sex With a Real Person – Gary Wilson – SC 171," The Relationship School (podcast), November 1, 2017, https://relationshipschool.net/podcast/porn-and-relationships-gary-wilson-sc-171/.

253. This quote is from Philip Berk's website, https://philipmberk.com/index.php/about/.

254. Dan B. Allender (with Traci Mullins), *Healing the Wounded Heart: The Heartache of Sexual Abuse and the Hope of Transformation* (Grand Rapids, MI: Baker Books, 2016), 25 (Kindle edition).

255. Allender, *Healing the Wounded Heart*, 48.

256. Russell Brand, *Recovery: Freedom from Our Addictions* (New York: Henry Holt and Company, 2017), 37 (Kindle edition).

257. Dr. Harvey Schwartz, personal interview, 2018.

258. Tanya Burleson, personal interview, 2014.

259. Andrew B. Newberg and Mark Robert Waldman, *How Enlightenment Changes Your Brain: The New Science of Transformation* (New York: Avery, 2016).

260. Candice Feiring, Lynn Taska, and Michael Lewis, "A process model for understanding adaptation to sexual abuse: The role of shame in defining stigmatization," *Child Abuse & Neglect* 20, no. 8 (1996) 767-82, http://iapsac.org/wp-content/uploads/2014/10/A-process-model-for-understanding-adaptation-to-sexual-abuse-The-role-of-shame-in-defining-stigmatization.pdf.

261. Schwartz, personal interview, 2018.

262. Gene McConnell, personal interview, 2018.

263. Allender, *Healing the Wounded Heart*, 48.

264. Dr. Kristin Neff is an associate professor of educational psychology at the University of Texas. Her insights are from an article titled "The Motivational Power of Self-Compassion," posted on her website, Self-Compassion.org. See https://self-compassion.org/the-motivational-power-of-self-compassion.

265. Allender, *Healing the Wounded Heart*, 46.

266. Allender, *Healing the Wounded Heart*, 48.

267. Jerome E. Groopman, *The Anatomy of Hope: How You Can Find Strength in the Face of Illness* (New York: Pocket Books, 2006) xvi.

268. Dr. Robert Leahy, "How to Overcome Your Feelings of Hopelessness," Oprah.com, August 5, 2010, https://www.oprah.com/spirit/how-to-overcome-your-feelings-of-hopelessness/.

269. Henri Nouwen, quoted in R. Wayne Willis, *Hope Notes: 52 Meditations to Nudge Your World*, (Louisville, KY: Westminster John Knox Press, 2004).

270. Kevin B. Skinner, *Treating Pornography Addiction: The Essential Tools for Recovery* (Orem, UT: GrowthClimate, 2005), Kindle edition, locations 1066-1077.

271. E. M. Dawson, "Understanding and Predicting College Students' Alcohol Use: Influence of Attitudes and Subjective Norms," *Dissertation Abstracts International* 61, no. 3 (2000): 1320B.

272. Stanton Peele, *7 Tools to Beat Addiction: A New Path to Recovery from Addictions of Any Kind: Smoking, Alcohol, Food, Drugs, Gambling, Sex, Love* (New York: Three Rivers Press, 2004) 27 (Kindle edition).

273. J. S. Park, *Cutting It Off: Breaking Porn Addiction and How to Quit for Good* (Tampa, FL: The Way Everlasting Ministry, 2018), 44 (Kindle edition).

274. Elliot Berkman, quoted in Cassie Shortsleeve, "5 Science-Approved Ways to Break a Bad Habit," *TIME*, August 28, 2018, http://time.com/5373528/break-bad-habit-science/.

275. Berkman/Shortsleeve, "5 Science-Approved Ways to Break a Bad Habit."

276. Matt Peplinski, *Sex Addiction Cure: How to Overcome Porn Addiction and Sexual Compulsion*, (Tczew, Poland: PsychoTao, 2017), 45-46.

277. J. Cumming and S. E. Williams, "The role of imagery in performance," in Shane M. Murphy (editor), *The Oxford Handbook of Sport and Performance Psychology* (New York: Oxford University Press, 2012), 213–232; and J. Hardy, "Speaking clearly: A critical review of the self-talk literature," *Psychology of Sport and Exercise* 7 (2006): 81–97. See also, McCullagh, Law, and Sainte-Marie, "Modeling and performance," in *The Oxford Handbook of Sports Performance Psychology*, pages 250-272; Sainte-Marie, Law, Rymal, Hall, and McCullagh, "Observation interventions for motor skill learning and performance: An applied model for the use of observation," *International Review of Sport and Exercise Psychology* 5, (2012):145–176; and C. Wakefield and D. Smith, "Perfecting practice: Applying the PETTLEP Model of Motor Imagery," *Journal of Sport Psychology in Action* 3 (2012): 1–11.

278. Peter Gollwitzer, "A Psychology Professor Reveals How to Break Bad Habits Once and for All," *Fortune*, January 25, 2017, http://fortune.com/2017/01/25/how-to-break-bad-habits-2/.

279. Ibid.

280. Ibid.

281. Ibid.

282. David Strayer, quoted in Jill Suttie, "How Nature Can Make You Kinder, Happier, and More Creative," *Greater Good Magazine*, March 2, 2016, https://greatergood.berkeley.edu/article/item/how_nature_makes_you_kinder_happier_more_creative.

283. Ellen Crean, "He Took a Bullet for Reagan," *CBS News*, June 11, 2004, www.cbsnews.com/news/he-took-a-bullet-for-reagan/.

284. David T. Neal, Wendy Wood, Mengju Wu, and David Kurlander. "The Pull of the Past: When Do Habits Persist Despite Conflict With Motives?" *Personality and Social Psychology Bulletin* 37, (2011, No. 37): 1428.

285. Pauling, personal interview.

286. Swiss, personal interview.

287. B.Y. Goldstein, J.K. Steinberg, G. Avnalem, and P.R. Kerndt, "High Chlamydia and Gonorrhea Incidence and Reinfection Among Performers in the Adult Film Industry," *Sexually Transmitted Diseases*, 2011; 38(7). See also the article titled "Uncovering the Realities of STI Testing in the Porn Industry," posted August 17, 2021, on the website fightthenewdrug.org. (Editor's note: In August and October of 2021, the adult film industry announced two HIV-related production holds.)

288. Andrew Ferebee, *The Porn Pandemic: A Simple Guide to Understanding and Ending Pornography Addiction for Men* (San Diego, CA: Knowledge for Men LLC, 2016), Kindle locations 907-930.

289. Sheri Keffer, *Intimate Deception: Healing the Wounds of Sexual Betrayal* (Grand Rapids, MI: Baker Publishing Group, 2018), 22 (Kindle edition).

290. Barb DePree, "What to Do When Your Partner Is Addicted to Porn," HealthyWomen, August 18, 2017, www.healthywomen.org/content/article/what-do-when-your-partner-addicted-porn.

291. Ethan Kross et al., "Social rejection shares somatosensory representations with physical pain," *PNAS* 108, no. 15 (April 2011) http://selfcontrol.psych.lsa.umich.edu/wp-content/uploads/2013/09/2011_3_Kross_etal_PNAS1.pdf.

292. Robert Weiss, "Understanding Relationship, Sexual, and Intimate Betrayal as Trauma (PTSD)," Psych Central (blog), September 26, 2012, https://psychcentral.com/blog/sex/2012/09/understanding-relationship-sexual-and-intimate-betrayal-as-trauma-ptsd.

293. Berit Brogaard, "Why Is Infidelity So Painful?" *Psychology Today*, January 16, 2016, https://www.psychologytoday.com/us/blog/the-mysteries-love/201601/why-is-infidelity-so-painful.

294. Quote source: https://quotes.thefamouspeople.com/terry-goodkind-2969.php

295. Barbara Steffens, PhD, and Marsha Means, *Your Sexually Addicted Spouse: How Partners Can Cope and Heal* (Liberty Corner, NJ: New Horizon Press, 2021), 20 (Kindle edition).

296. For a comprehensive look at trauma, see, https://www.apa.org/topics/trauma/.

297. Steffens and Means, *Your Sexually Addicted Spouse*, 11.

298. Steffens and Means, *Your Sexually Addicted Spouse*, 4-5.

299. Sheri Keffer, Intimate Deception Betrayal Trauma (IDBT) ™, as explained on her website, drsherikeffer.com.

300. Steffens and Means, *Your Sexually Addicted Spouse*, 6-7.

301. This quote is from Helen Keller's 1903 essay "Optimism," which has been published in a variety of collections.

302. William Goodwin, "Q&A: Jerry Cantrell of Alice in Chains," Spin, August 21, 2009, https://www.spin.com/2009/08/qa-jerry-cantrell-alice-chains/.

303. "AA, Al-Anon owe debt of gratitude to Lois Wilson," (undated article), Hazelden Betty Ford Foundation, https://www.hazelden.org/web/public/ade50711.page.

304. Steffens and Means, *Your Sexually Addicted Spouse*, 167.

305. Steffens and Means, *Your Sexually Addicted Spouse*, 25-27.

306. Steffens and Means, *Your Sexually Addicted Spouse*, 28-29.

307. "Self-worth," Dictionary.com, accessed November 24, 2021, https://www.dictionary.com/browse/self-worth.

308. Brogaard, "Why Is Infidelity So Painful?

309. Robert Enright, *Forgiveness Is a Choice: A Step-By-Step Process for Resolving Anger and Restoring Hope* (Washington, DC: American Psychological Association [APA LifeTools], 2001), 25.

310. Barbara A. Elliott, "Forgiveness Therapy: A Clinical Intervention for Chronic Disease," *Journal of Religion and Health*, 50, no. 2 (June 2011): 240-247. Retrieved from http://www.jstor.org/stable/41349784.

311. S. R. Freedman and R. D. Enright, "Forgiveness as an intervention goal with incest survivors," *Journal of Consulting and Clinical Psychology* 64, no. 5 (1996): 983-992.

312. Steffens and Means, *Your Sexually Addicted Spouse*, 172-173.

313. Schwartz, personal interview, 2018.

314. Ben Franklin coined this quote in 1736 while advising the city of Philadelphia that preventing fires was preferable to fighting them. See https://www.cam.ac.uk/research/news/ounce-of-prevention-pound-of-cure.

315. David Cameron, "The Internet and Pornography: Prime Minister Calls for Action," speech transcription, Gov.uk, July 22, 2013, https://www.gov.uk/government/speeches/the-internet-and-pornography-prime-minister-calls-for-action. For critiques of Cameron's efforts, see Keith Wagstaff, "Why Britain's new porn ban is a dumb idea," January 8, 2015, https://theweek.com/articles/461911/why-britains-new-porn-ban-dumb-idea; and James Temperton, "How David Cameron's clean web crusade created the porn block," Wired, October 4, 2019, https://www.wired.co.uk/article/porn-block-analysis-good-clean-internet.

316. Alfie Kohn, *Unconditional Parenting: Moving from Rewards and Punishments to Love and Reason* (New York: Atria Books, 2006), page number n/a.

317. Gavin de Becker, *The Gift of Fear: Survival Signals That Protect Us from Violence* (London: Bloomsbury, 1997), 25-42.

318. Gail Dines, in an interview with Stephen M. Deusner, *Washington Post*, July 14, 2010. https://www.washingtonpost.com/express/wp/2010/07/15/gail-dines-how-pornland-hijacked-our-sexuality-politics-prose/?noredirect=on&utm_term=.928f43e82bcf.

319. Maya Angelou's *I Know Why the Caged Bird Sings* was first published by Random House in 1969.

320. Kidsmatter, "Promoting mental health in early childhood," Kidsmatter.edu.au, accessed Nov. 21, 2018, https://www.kidsmatter.edu.au/mental-health-matters/mental-health-basics-promoting-mental-health/risk-and-protective-factors-early.

321. National Center for Mental Health Promotion and Violence Prevention, "Risk and Resilience 101," July 2004, http://www.promoteprevent.org/sites/www.promoteprevent.org/files/resources/Risk%20and%20Resilience.pdf.

322. Harvard University Center on the Developing Child, "InBrief: The Science of Resilience," 2015, https://developingchild.harvard.edu/science/key-concepts/resilience/.

323. Harvard University Center on the Developing Child, "Resilience," 2015, https://developingchild.harvard.edu/wp-content/uploads/2015/05/The-Science-of-Resilience.pdf .

324. Jack Shonkoff, "Supportive Relationships and Active Skill-Building Strengthen the Foundations of Resilience," National Scientific Council on the Developing Child, May 2015. https://developingchild.harvard.edu/science/key-concepts/resilience/.

325. Ken Rotenberg, *Interpersonal Trust During Childhood and Adolescence* (Boston: Cambridge University Press, 2012).

326. C. Cole, P. L. Harris, and M.A. Koenig, "Entitled to Trust? Philosophical Frameworks and Evidence from Children," *Analyse & Kritik* 34, (2012): 195-216; and M. A. Koenig and E. Stephens, "Characterizing Children's Responsiveness to Cues of Speaker Trustworthiness: Two Proposals," in E. Robinson and S. Einav (editors) *Trust and Skepticism: Children's Selective Learning from Testimony* (Cambridge, UK: Psychology Press, 2014).

327. Melissa Koenig, Paul Harris, and Fabrice Clement, "Trust in Testimony; Children's Use of True and False Statements," Kellogg School of Management at Northwestern University, October 1, 2004. https://www.kellogg.northwestern.edu/trust-project/videos/koenig-how-children-gauge-trustworthiness-key-findings.aspx.

328. Douglas S., personal interview.

329. Media Literacy Now, "What is Media Literacy?" Media Literacy Project, accessed January 30, 2018, and May 13, 2022, https://medialiteracynow.org/what-is-media-literacy/.

330. Douglas Kellner and Jeff Share, "Critical Media Literacy, Democracy, and the Reconstruction of Education," March 2, 2007, https://pages.gseis.ucla.edu/faculty/kellner/essays/2007_Kellner-Share-Steinberg%20and%20Macedo_ch1.pdf.

331. Michael Margolis quote source: https://twitter.com/natgeoeducation/status/1144183742623338496?lang=bg.

332. Chris Hedges, "Resistance Is the Supreme Act of Faith," Truthdig, December 31, 2018, https://www.truthdig.com/articles/resistance-is-the-supreme-act-of-faith/.

333. For more information on US and international anti-tobacco efforts, see www.scientificamerican.com/article/anti-tobacco-efforts-have-saved-millions-of-lives-worldwide/.

334. This quote from Lincoln is from his first debate with Stephen A. Douglas in Ottawa, Illinois, August 21, 1858.

335. Sarah Ditum and Amelia Tait, "Should internet porn be banned?" *Prospect Magazine*, December 13, 2018 (and updated in February 2019), https://www.prospectmagazine.co.uk/magazine/should-internet-porn-be-banned.

336. "Concurrent Resolution on the Public Health Crisis," 2016 General Session, State of Utah, https://le.utah.gov/~2016/bills/static/scr009.html.
    Editor's note: Gary Herbert served as Utah governor from 2009 to 2021.

337. Robert Jensen, "What Is Sex For?" Culture Reframed, August 27, 2017, https://www.culturereframed.org/what-is-sex-for-robert-jensen/.

338. John T. Chirban, "Purposes of Sex: Setting an honest tone about sex from the start," *Psychology Today*, July 29, 2013, https://www.psychologytoday.com/blog/age-un-innocence/201307/purposes-sex.

339. William M. Struthers, *Wired for Intimacy: How Pornography Hijacks the Male Brain* (Downers Grove, IL: IVP Books, 2009); and Peter Benson, Kathleen Kovner Kline, et al., "Hardwired to Connect," Commission on Children at Risk, Institute for American Values, 2003, https://www.ojp.gov/ncjrs/virtual-library/abstracts/hardwired-connect-new-scientific-case-authoritative-communities.

340. Robert Jensen, "What Is Sex For?" Culture Reframed, August 24, 2017, https://www.culturereframed.org/what-is-sex-for-robert-jensen/.

341. Melissa Farley, Ann Cotton, Jacqueline Lynne, Sybille Zumbeck, Frida Spiwak, Maria E. Reyes, Dinorah Alvarez, and Ufuk Sesgini (2003) "Prostitution and Posttraumatic Stress Disorder: An update on violence and posttraumatic stress disorder," *Journal of Trauma Practice* 2, Numbers 3 and 4, 33-74.

Printed in Great Britain
by Amazon

21103396R00147